Stock Market Investing Strategies

A Detailed Beginner's Guide on How to Trade in the Stock Market. Learn Secret Investment Strategies for Investing and Start to Make Money

Matthew Aziz

Published by: Matthew Aziz

TABLE OF CONTENTS

Introduction

Stock is a term used to symbolize an investor's ownership in a company. Those who own stock are commonly called stockholders or shareholders. As a shareholder, an investor theoretically owns a percentage of everything the company owns or owes. The company's profitability, or lack thereof, determines whether its stock is traded at a higher or lower price. While trading of debt and commodities has its origins in the Middle Ages, the modern concept of a stock market began in the late 16th century.

Origins Of Stock

Stock markets were started when countries in the New World began trading with each other. While many pioneer merchants wanted to start huge businesses, this required substantial amounts of capital that no single merchant could raise alone. As a result, groups of investors pooled their savings and became business partners and co-owners with individual shares in their businesses to form joint-stock companies. Originated by the Dutch, joint-stock companies became a viable business model for many struggling businesses. In 1602, the Dutch East India Co. issued the first paper shares. This exchangeable medium allowed shareholders to conveniently buy, sell, and trade their stock with other shareholders and investors.

Significance

The idea was so successful that the selling of shares spread to other maritime powers such as Portugal, Spain, and France. Eventually, the practice found its way to England. Trade with the New World was big business so trading ventures were initiated. Other industries during the Industrial Revolution began using the idea as a way to generate start-up capital. This influx of capital allowed for the discovery and development of the New World and the growth of modern industrialized manufacturing.

History Of The Stock Market

As the volume of shares increased, the need for an organized marketplace to exchange these shares became necessary. As a result, stock traders decided to meet at a London coffeehouse, which they used as a marketplace. Eventually, they took over the coffeehouse and, in 1773, changed its name to the "stock exchange." Thus, the first exchange, the London Stock Exchange, was founded. The idea made its way to the American colonies with an exchange started in Philadelphia in 1790.

The First Stock Exchange – Sans The Stock

Belgium boasted a stock exchange as far back as 1531 in Antwerp. Brokers and moneylenders would meet there to deal with business, government, and even individual debt issues. It is odd to think of a stock exchange that dealt exclusively in promissory notes and bonds, but in the 1500s there were no real stocks. There were many flavors of business-financier partnerships that produced income as stocks do, but there was no official share that changed hands.

Impact

Today, there are many stock exchanges worldwide, each supplying the capital necessary to support industry growth. Without these vital funds, many revolutionary ideas would never become a reality, nor would fundamental improvements be made to existing products. Besides, the stock market creates personal wealth and financial stability through private investment, allowing individuals to fund their retirement and or other ventures.

Understanding The Stock Market

While today it is possible to purchase almost everything online, there is usually a designated market for every commodity. For instance, people drive to city outskirts and farmlands to purchase Christmas trees, visit the local timber market to buy wood and other necessary material for home furniture and renovations, and go to stores like Walmart for their regular grocery supplies.

Such dedicated markets serve as a platform where numerous buyers and sellers meet, interact, and transact. Since the number of market participants is huge, one is assured of a fair price. For example, if there is only one seller of Christmas trees in the entire city, he will have the liberty to charge any price he pleases as the buyers won't have anywhere else to go. If the number of tree sellers is large in a common marketplace, they will have to compete against each other to attract buyers. The buyers will be spoiled for choice with low- or optimum-pricing making it a fair market with price transparency. Even while shopping online, buyers compare prices offered by different sellers on the same shopping portal or across different portals to get the best deals, forcing the various online sellers to offer the best price.

A stock market is a similar designated market for trading various kinds of securities in a controlled, secure, and managed the environment. Since the stock market brings together hundreds of thousands of market participants who wish to buy and sell shares, it ensures fair pricing practices and transparency in transactions. While earlier stock markets used to issue and deal with paper-based physical share certificates, the modern-day computer-aided stock markets operate electronically.

Chapter 1 - What Is Stock Market?

Even if you have a retirement account or other investment portfolio, you might be confused about what the stock market is. So let's sort it out.

A stock market is a place where just about anyone can invest in a company by buying "shares." Buying a share makes you a partial owner in a company, although you won't get to make decisions about how the business is run. Once a business is listed on a stock market and investors start buying shares, you can imagine that the business is broken up into thousands of tiny parts.

The stock market refers to public markets that exist for issuing, buying, and selling stocks that trade on a stock exchange or over-the-counter. Stocks, also known as equities, represent fractional ownership in a company, and a stock market is a place where investors can buy and sell ownership of such investible assets. An efficiently functioning stock market is considered critical to economic development, as it gives companies the ability to quickly access capital from the public.

What Exactly Is The Stock Market?

The terms "stock market" and "stock exchange" are sometimes used interchangeably. In the U.S., there are two major stock exchanges or locations that stocks are traded. Both are in New

York City: the New York Stock Exchange on Wall Street and the Nasdaq, which is located in Times Square. A company will usually list its shares for trading on one of the exchanges, but not both.

Companies that are traded on a stock market are usually established enough to be serious players in their industry. A company gets onto the stock market through an initial public offering, or IPO, which are the first shares it sells beyond any private investors who provide funds to get the company started or help to help it grow. If a company is doing well and its stock is popular, the price goes up. If the economy isn't doing so hot or that company has a bad day in the press, the price may go down. These fluctuations impact how much your share of that company that you already bought is worth in your portfolio. If you decide to sell your shares when the stock price is up, you may get more money in the sale than you initially paid. If the stock price is down when you sell, there's a chance you'll lose money.

What Is The Stock Exchange Market?

The traditional medium where stocks or shares, bonds, and other securities are exchanged between a stock and a trader. The stock exchange, also known as bourse or Stock Market in Nigeria, can provide facilities for the issue and redemption of financial instruments with the inclusion of the payment of income and dividends. Other assets listed on the stock exchange can include, unity trusts, bonds, and pooled investment products.

What Is A Stock Market Exactly?

A stock market is a place where the shares of companies that are publicly owned can be bought and sold either OTC (Over-The-Counter) or through centralized exchanges. The equity stock market, as it is also known by, has established itself as a free-market economy, in that it offers companies the ability to access capital in exchange for offering interested outside parties a portion in the ownership of the company. The stock market or equity market offers opportunities to investors to increase their income without the high risk of entering into their businesses with high overheads and startup costs. On the other hand, selling of stocks did help the companies themselves expand exponentially. When you purchase a company's shares it is generally associated with the increase in the company's worth.

Therefore, trading on the stock or equity markets can be a win-win for both investor and owner. There is a negative risk however small or large depending on the amount of stock bought, that one can lose money in a trading environment. If the stocks traders hold from the company lose value, then so does the trader. If he decides to sell his stocks when the value is lower, he will sell at a loss.

How Has Stock Exchange Market Broken Down?

There are various segments of the stock market to consider when entering into a purchase or interest in the shares of a particular public company. There are two sections that the stock exchange market can be divided into the primary market and the secondary market.

Primary Market The market where securities are initially created. This is an open stock market where a company's shares are offered and sold for the first time and directly from the company issuing them. Having precedence as a primary listed company that lends to a company's credibility and therefore opens doors to investors being more predisposed to purchasing shares in that company. The primary exchange market is dominated by larger investment institutes such as investment banks, hedge funds, etc.

Secondary Market In the secondary market investors trade these stocks themselves and the company that had previously sold the stock initially is not a direct participant in the transaction. Selling and buying of shares that are already owned by investors is the typical idea of the stock market, even though stocks are also sold on the primary market as this is the stage they are initially issued from.

OTC Market The OTC market, also known in trading as the off-exchange, is an option for investors to take part in the purchasing and selling of stock from a decentralized market. Decentralized is where a transaction of buying or selling will take place between two parties, such as the trader and the broker. Transactions are generally done electronically either telephonically, through email or via a trading platform, and not through the local stock exchange. The OTC market is usually for stocks and stock prices not commonly listed on the stock exchange.

How To Invest In The Stock Exchange Market?

Besides the obvious, investing in a certain company's stocks and trading, several alternative ways can be conducted when trading to establishing a strategy on trading stocks, with the possibility of making a profit with a company's shares as an investment choice.

Value Investing: This is a simple investment strategy, where certain stocks that are selected trade for a lesser amount of their inherent value. These types of investors (value investors) actively seek out undervalued stocks as they believe they will see returns on these listings. This type of investing does not require you to have a background in finance, however, an understanding of trading and basic finance knowledge is recommended when entering into any trading or purchasing of stocks.

Price-Earnings Ratio P/E: Ratio as it is better known in short is defined as a company's measure on its current share price relative to its per-share earnings. This is how they calculate the price-earnings ratio:

By taking the stock price of the company and dividing it by is earnings per share (EPS) = market value per share. The P/E ratio is a dollar amount that a trader can expect to invest in a company to receive one dollar of that company's earnings.

Dividend-Paying Stock: Dividends are a way that companies reward shareholders for owning a stock in their company. Dividends are generally paid in cash every quarter and can become a steady payment if the investment taken is fruitful, while this can develop another opportunity in itself to purchase additional stocks. This is a longer-term investment with a lower risk, as these companies are generally more financially stable and overtime dividends rise and they are committed to dividend payments on their companies' stocks.

Shares Trading Market

Swing Trading Swing trading has become a very popular way to trade in the short-term when trading stocks and trading options. Lasting less than one day generally, swing trader's positions can last up to two weeks. When swing trading, the goal is to identify the overall trend and 'swing in' and capture the gains while the markets are on a trend. The use of the is advantageous when swing trading to monitor quick market changes as and when they happen.

Day Trading Speculating on a buy or a sell of a particular share, commodity, index, or currency that takes place strictly only on the same day. Positions can be opened the second the markets open or throughout the day however, all positions must be closed before the market closes for that trading day. Traders that use this trading strategy are known as day traders. Depending on the type of trader you are be it longer or shorter-term, any trading in the short term will have more profit as well as the risk of loss potential. It is fast and trades are entered into and exited in a short period.

Two Basic Approaches To Stock Market Investing

There are countless methods of stock picking that analysts and investors employ, but virtually all of them are one form or another of the two basic stock buying strategies of value investing or growth investing.

1. Value investors typically invest in well-established companies that have shown steady profitability over a long period and may offer regular dividend income. Value investing is more focused on avoiding risk than growth investing is, although value investors do seek to buy stocks when they consider the stock price to be an undervalued bargain.

2. Growth investors seek out companies with exceptionally high growth potential, hoping to realize maximum appreciation in the share price. They are usually less concerned with dividend income and are more willing to risk investing in relatively young companies. Technology stocks, because of their high growth potential, are often favored by growth investors.

Purposes Of The Stock Market – Capital And Investment Income

The stock market serves two very important purposes. The first is to provide capital to companies that they can use to fund and expand their businesses. If a company issues one million shares of stock that initially sell for $10 a share, then that provides the company with $10 million of capital that it can use to grow its business (minus whatever fees the company pays for an investment bank to manage the stock offering). By offering stock shares instead of borrowing the capital needed for expansion, the company avoids incurring debt and paying interest charges on that debt.

The secondary purpose the stock market serves is to give investors – those who purchase stocks – the opportunity to share in the profits of publicly-traded companies. Investors can profit from stock buying in one of two ways. Some stocks pay regular dividends (a given amount of money per share of stock someone owns). The other way investors can profit from buying stocks is by selling their stock for a profit if the stock price increases from their purchase price. For example, if an investor buys shares of a company's stock at $10 a share and the price of the stock subsequently rises to $15 a share, the investor can then realize a 50% profit on their investment by selling their shares.

How Stocks Are Traded – Exchanges And OTC

Most stocks are traded on exchanges such as the New York Stock Exchange (NYSE) or the NASDAQ. Stock exchanges essentially provide the marketplace to facilitate the buying and selling of stocks among investors. Stock exchanges are regulated by government agencies, such as the Securities and Exchange Commission (SEC) in the United States, that oversees the market to protect investors from financial fraud and to keep the exchange market functioning smoothly.

Although the vast majority of stocks are traded on exchanges, some stocks are traded over-the-counter (OTC), where buyers and sellers of stocks commonly trade through a dealer, or "market maker", who specifically deals with the stock. OTC stocks are stocks that do not meet the minimum price or other requirements for being listed on exchanges.

OTC stocks are not subject to the same public reporting regulations as stocks listed on exchanges, so it is not as easy for investors to obtain reliable information on the companies issuing such stocks. Stocks in the OTC market are typically much more thinly traded than exchange-traded stocks, which means that investors often must deal with large spreads between bid and ask prices for an OTC stock. In contrast, exchange-traded stocks are much more liquid, with relatively small bid-ask spreads.

Analyzing Stocks – Market Cap, EPS, And Financial Ratios

Stock market analysts and investors may look at a variety of factors to indicate a stock's probable future direction, up or down in price. Here's a rundown on some of the most commonly viewed variables for stock analysis. A stock's market capitalization, or market cap, is the total value of all the outstanding shares of the stock. A higher market capitalization usually indicates a company that is more well-established and financially sound.

Publicly traded companies are required by exchange regulatory bodies to regularly provide earnings reports. These reports, issued quarterly and annually, are carefully watched by market analysts as a good indicator of how well a company's business is doing. Among the key factors analyzed from earnings reports are the company's earnings per share (EPS), which reflects the company's profits as divided among all of its outstanding shares of stock.

Analysts and investors also frequently examine several financial ratios that are intended to indicate the financial stability, profitability, and growth potential of a publicly-traded company. The following are a few of the key financial ratios that investors and analysts consider:

1. Price To Earnings (P/E) Ratio: The ratio of a company's stock price about its EPS. A higher P/E ratio indicates that investors are willing to pay higher prices per share for the company's stock because they expect the company to grow and the stock price to rise.

2. Debt To Equity Ratio: This is a fundamental metric of a company's financial stability, as it shows what percentage of a company's operations are being funded by debt compared to what percentage is being funded by equity investors. A lower debt to equity ratio, indicating primary funding from investors, is preferable.

3. Return On Equity (ROE) Ratio: The return on equity (ROE) ratio is considered a good indicator of a company's growth potential, as it shows the company's net income relative to the total equity investment in the company.

4. Profit Margin: There are several profit margin ratios that investors may consider, including operating profit margin and net profit margin. The advantage of looking at profit margin instead of just an absolute dollar profit figure is that it shows what a company's percentage profitability is. For example, a company may show a profit of $2 million, but if that only translates to a 3% profit margin, then any significant decline in revenues may threaten the company's profitability.

Other commonly used financial ratios include return on assets (ROA), dividend yield, price to book (P/B) ratio, current ratio, and the inventory turnover ratio.

How The Stock Market Works

In a nutshell, stock markets provide a secure and regulated environment where market participants can transact in shares and other eligible financial instruments with confidence with zero- to low-operational risk. Operating under the defined rules as stated by the regulator, the stock markets act as primary markets and as secondary markets.

As a primary market, the stock market allows companies to issue and sell their shares to the common public for the first time through the process of initial public offerings (IPO). This activity helps companies raise the necessary capital from investors. It essentially means that a company divides itself into several shares (say, 20 million shares) and sells a part of those shares (say, 5 million shares) to the common public at a price (say, $10 per share).

To facilitate this process, a company needs a marketplace where these shares can be sold. This marketplace is provided by the stock market. If everything goes as per the plans, the company will successfully sell the 5 million shares for $10 per share and collect $50 million worth of funds. Investors will get the company shares which they can expect to hold for their preferred duration, in anticipation of rising in share price and any potential income in the form of dividend payments. The stock exchange acts as a facilitator for this capital raising process and receives a fee for its services from the company and its financial partners.

Following the first-time share issuance IPO exercise called the listing process, the stock exchange also serves as the trading platform that facilitates regular buying and selling of the listed shares. This constitutes the secondary market. The stock exchange earns a fee for every trade that occurs on its platform during the secondary market activity.

The stock exchange shoulders the responsibility of ensuring price transparency, liquidity, price discovery, and fair dealings in such trading activities. As almost all major stock markets across the globe now operate electronically, the exchange maintains trading systems that efficiently manage the buy and sell orders from various market participants. They perform the price matching function to facilitate trade execution at a price fair to both buyers and sellers.

A listed company may also offer new, additional shares through other offerings at a later stage, like through rights issues or follow-on offers. They may even buyback or delist their shares. The stock exchange facilitates such transactions. The stock exchange often creates and maintains various market-level and sector-specific indicators, like the S&P 500 index or Nasdaq 100 index, which provide a measure to track the movement of the overall market. Other methods include the Stochastic Oscillator and Stochastic Momentum Index. The stock exchanges also maintain all company news, announcements, and financial reporting, which can be usually accessed on their official websites. A stock exchange also supports various other corporate-level, transaction-related activities. For instance, profitable companies may reward investors by paying dividends which usually comes from a part of the company's earnings. The exchange maintains all such information and may support its processing to a certain extent.

Functions Of A Stock Market

A stock market primarily serves the following functions:

1. Fair Dealing In Securities Transactions: Depending on the standard rules of demand and supply, the stock exchange needs to ensure that all interested market participants have instant access to data for all buy and sell orders thereby helping in the fair and transparent pricing of securities. Additionally, it should also perform efficient matching of appropriate buy and sell orders.

For example, there may be three buyers who have placed orders for buying Microsoft shares at $100, $105 and $110, and there may be four sellers who are willing to sell Microsoft shares at

$110, $112, $115 and $120. The exchange (through their computer operated automated trading systems) needs to ensure that the best buy and best sell are matched, which in this case is at $110 for the given quantity of trade.

2. Efficient Price Discovery: Stock markets need to support an efficient mechanism for price discovery, which refers to the act of deciding the proper price of a security and is usually performed by assessing market supply and demand and other factors associated with the transactions.

Say, a U.S.-based software company is trading for $100 and has a market capitalization of $5 billion. A news item comes in that the EU regulator has imposed a fine of $2 billion on the company which essentially means that 40 percent of the company's value may be wiped out. While the stock market may have imposed a trading price range of $90 and $110 on the company's share price, it should efficiently change the permissible trading price limit to accommodate for the possible changes in the share price, else shareholders may struggle to trade at a fair price.

3. Liquidity Maintenance: While getting the number of buyers and sellers for a particular financial security are out of control for the stock market, it needs to ensure that whosoever is qualified and willing to trade gets instant access to place orders which should get executed at the fair price.

4. Security And Validity Of Transactions: While more participants are important for the efficient working of a market, the same market needs to ensure that all participants are verified and remain compliant with the necessary rules and regulations, leaving no room for default by any of the parties. Additionally, it should ensure that all associated entities operating in the market must also adhere to the rules, and work within the legal framework given by the regulator.

5. Support All Eligible Types Of Participants: A marketplace is made by a variety of participants, which include market makers, investors, traders, speculators, and hedgers. All these participants operate in the stock market with different roles and functions. For instance, an investor may buy stocks and hold them for long term spanning many years, while a trader may enter and exit a position within seconds. A market maker provides necessary liquidity in the market, while a hedger may like to trade in derivatives for mitigating the risk involved in investments. The stock market should ensure that all such participants can operate seamlessly fulfilling their desired roles to ensure the market continues to operate efficiently.

6. Investor Protection: Along with wealthy and institutional investors, a very large number of small investors are also served by the stock market for their small amount of investments. These investors may have limited financial knowledge, and may not be fully aware of the pitfalls of investing in stocks and other listed instruments. The stock exchange must implement necessary measures to offer the necessary protection to such investors to shield them from financial loss and ensure customer trust.

For instance, a stock exchange may categorize stocks in various segments depending on their risk profiles and allow limited or no trading by common investors in high-risk stocks. Exchanges often impose restrictions to prevent individuals with limited income and knowledge from getting into risky bets of derivatives.

7. **Balanced Regulation:** Listed companies are largely regulated and their dealings are monitored by market regulators, like the Securities and Exchange Commission (SEC) of the U.S. Additionally, exchanges also mandate certain requirements – like, timely filing of quarterly financial reports and instant reporting of any relevant developments - to ensure all market participants become aware of corporate happenings. Failure to adhere to the regulations can lead to suspension of trading by the exchanges and other disciplinary measures.

Regulating The Stock Market

A local financial regulator or competent monetary authority or institute is assigned the task of regulating the stock market of a country. The Securities and Exchange Commission (SEC) is the regulatory body charged with overseeing the U.S. stock markets. The SEC is a federal agency that works independently of the government and political pressure. The mission of the SEC is stated as: "to protect investors, maintain fair, orderly, and efficient markets, and facilitate capital formation."

Stock Market Participants

Along with long-term investors and short term traders, there are many different types of players associated with the stock market. Each has a unique role, but many of the roles are intertwined and depend on each other to make the market run effectively.

Stockbrokers, also known as registered representatives in the U.S., are licensed professionals who buy and sell securities on behalf of investors. The brokers act as intermediaries between the stock exchanges and the investors by buying and selling stocks on the investors' behalf. An account with a retail broker is needed to gain access to the markets.

Portfolio managers are professionals who invest portfolios, or collections of securities, for clients. These managers get recommendations from analysts and make the buy or sell decisions for the portfolio. Mutual fund companies, hedge funds, and pension plans use portfolio managers to make decisions and set the investment strategies for the money they hold.

Investment bankers represent companies in various capacities, such as private companies that want to go public via an IPO or companies that are involved in pending mergers and acquisitions.

They take care of the listing process in compliance with the regulatory requirements of the stock market.

Custodian and depot service providers, which are institutions holding customers' securities for safekeeping to minimize the risk of their theft or loss, also operate in sync with the exchange to transfer shares to/from the respective accounts of transacting parties based on trading on the stock market.

Market Maker: A market maker is a broker-dealer who facilitates the trading of shares by posting bid and ask prices along with maintaining an inventory of shares. He ensures sufficient liquidity in the market for a particular (set of) share(s), and profits from the difference between the bid and the asking price he quotes.

How Stock Exchanges Make Money

Stock exchanges operate as for-profit institutes and charge a fee for their services. The primary source of income for these stock exchanges is the revenues from the transaction fees that are charged for each trade carried out on its platform. Additionally, exchanges earn revenue from the listing fee charged to companies during the IPO process and other follow-on offerings.

The exchange also earns from selling market data generated on its platform - like real-time data, historical data, summary data, and reference data – which is vital for equity research and other uses. Many exchanges will also sell technology products, like a trading terminal and dedicated network connection to the exchange, to the interested parties for a suitable fee.

The exchange may offer privileged services like high-frequency trading to larger clients like mutual funds and asset management companies (AMC), and earn money accordingly. There are provisions for regulatory fees and registration fees for different profiles of market participants, like the market maker and broker, which form other sources of income for the stock exchanges.

The exchange also makes profits by licensing their indexes (and their methodology) which are commonly used as a benchmark for launching various products like mutual funds and ETFs by AMCs. Many exchanges also provide courses and certification on various financial topics to industry participants and earn revenues from such subscriptions.

Competition For Stock Markets

While individual stock exchanges compete against each other to get maximum transaction volume, they are facing threat on two fronts.

1. Dark Pools: Dark pools, which are private exchanges or forums for securities trading and operate within private groups, are posing a challenge to public stock markets. Though their legal validity is subject to local regulations, they are gaining popularity as participants save big on transaction fees.

2. **Blockchain Ventures:** Amid rising popularity of blockchains, many crypto exchanges have emerged. Such exchanges are venues for trading cryptocurrencies and derivatives associated with that asset class. Though their popularity remains limited, they pose a threat to the traditional stock market model by automating a bulk of the work done by various stock market participants and by offering zero- to low-cost services.

Significance Of The Stock Market

The stock market is one of the most vital components of a free-market economy. It allows companies to raise money by offering stock shares and corporate bonds. It lets common investors participate in the financial achievements of the companies, make profits through capital gains, and earn money through dividends, although losses are also possible. While institutional investors and professional money managers do enjoy some privileges owing to their deep pockets, better knowledge, and higher risk-taking abilities, the stock market attempts to offer a level playing field to common individuals. The stock market works as a platform through which savings and investments of individuals are channelized into productive investment proposals. In the long term, it helps in capital formation & economic growth for the country.

The Beginnings Of The New York Stock Exchange

Enter the New York Stock Exchange (NYSE), established in 1792. Though not the first on U.S. soil – that honor goes to the Philadelphia Stock Exchange (PSE) – the NYSE rapidly grew to become the dominant stock exchange in the United States, and eventually in the world. The NYSE occupied a physically strategic position, located among some of the country's largest banks and companies, not to mention being situated in a major shipping port. The exchange established listing requirements for shares, and rather hefty fees initially, enabling it to quickly become a wealthy institution itself.

Where Is The Stock Market?

Two of the world's largest exchanges are in the United States: The Nasdaq and The New York Stock Exchange. Combined, they are worth around $21 trillion in market capitalization the value of all its shares.

Each exchange matches buyers with sellers, but they do it differently. The NYSE matches the highest bid for the lowest sales price, with a market maker for each stock who fills in the gap to ensure smooth trading. At the Nasdaq, buyers and sellers trade with a dealer instead of each other. It's done electronically, so trades happen in split seconds.

The United States is the world's financial capital because its financial markets are so sophisticated. As a result, information on companies is easy to obtain. This transparency increases the trust of investors from around the world. As a result, the U.S. stock market attracts more investors. That makes it even easier for a U.S. company to go public.

What Is A Stock Market Index?

The performance of the general U.S. stock market is tracked by its three principal indices: the Dow Jones Industrial Average or DJIA (stock prices of the top 30 U.S. companies), the S&P 500 (stocks of 500 large-cap U.S. companies), and the Nasdaq. Different components of the markets are also followed. For example, the Russell 2000 reports on 2,000 small-cap companies.

The major countries have their stock exchanges and indices. The five biggest: London, Tokyo, Shanghai, Hong Kong, and Euronext exchanges. Indices track various aspects of markets. For example, the MSCI Index tracks the performance of stocks in emerging market countries such as China, India, and Brazil.

Why Invest In The Stock Market?

The stock market contributes to the U.S. economy. Investors who believe the economy is growing will invest in stocks because a strong economy helps companies improve their earnings. It usually occurs along with the expansion phase of the business cycle. This is known as a bull market, which typically lasts two to five years.

Most of the stocks traded are common stocks. But some investors buy preferred stocks. They pay an agreed-upon dividend at regular intervals and they don't have voting rights. They are less risky but they also offer a smaller return. Stock market investing is considered the best way to achieve returns that beat inflation over time, and the returns, on average, outpace those of other investments, such as bonds or commodities.

You can make money in two ways through trading and by holding. Some investors prefer to let their stock appreciate over time, and many companies also give a dividend payment each year to the stockholders, which provides extra value. And unlike real estate, it's easy to buy stocks and just as easy to sell.

Risks Of Stock Market Investing

The most significant downside is that you can lose your entire investment if the stock price falls to zero. If the company goes bankrupt, stock investors are paid after bondholders. For that reason, stock investing can be an emotional rollercoaster.

Fees can take a big bite out of your investment as well, and the potential for fraud is a serious concern. If investors think the economy is slowing or stagnant, they may instead invest in bonds, which are a safer investment, although they do come with their risks. Bonds give a fixed return over the life of the loan and typically do well during the contraction phase of the business cycle.

When stock market prices decline less than 10%, that's known as a stock market correction. When prices fall that much or more in one day, it's known as a stock market crash. A bad crash could even cause a recession. The history of stock market crashes shows this is a frequent occurrence. When prices fall 20% or more, it's known as a bear market. These usually last 18 months.

How To Invest In The Stock Market

There are at least eight ways for you to invest in the stock market.

The quickest and least expensive (although time-consuming to research) is to buy stocks online. Online or "discount" brokers like E-Trade, SoFi, or TD Ameritrade might not charge a fee, or charge fees only for certain types of orders.

- ❖ If you need more guidance at a reasonable price, join an investment club, which is a group of people who research and invest together.
- ❖ A full-service broker will cost more but could be worth the price. He or she will give you professional recommendations and works at a large brokerage house.
- ❖ Large investment banks, like Goldman Sachs or Bank of America Merrill Lynch, can provide financial planning in addition to executing trades.
- ❖ A money manager charges the most but will do all the work for you.
- ❖ Fee-only financial advisors charge an annual fee, usually 1% of assets, and can provide advice on selecting investments, or may trade for you.
- ❖ Instead of buying individual stocks, you could buy them as part of an index fund or mutual fund.
- ❖ The riskiest is a hedge fund. They may also invest in derivatives, which could increase the return but will also increase the risk.
- ❖ Research any investment professional you're considering hiring, to help prevent losing your money through fraud.

Other Types Of Financial Markets

The stock market is just one type of financial market. Before you invest, make sure you are familiar with them all:

- Commodities are usually traded in futures options, which makes them more complicated. They include grains, oil, and the strangely-named pork bellies.
- Foreign exchange is where people buy and sell currencies. It's very high risk because the values can change dramatically for no apparent reason and change very quickly.
- Derivatives are very complicated securities that derive their value from the underlying asset, such as subprime mortgages. Individual investors should stay away. Even though they can offer huge returns, they can also deplete your entire life savings in a day.

Chapter 2 - The Key To Stock Investing

Ten Things to Consider Before You Make Investing Decisions

Given recent market events, you may be wondering whether you should make changes to your investment portfolio. The SEC's Office of Investor Education and Advocacy is concerned that some investors, including bargain hunters and mattress stuffers, are making rapid investment decisions without considering their long-term financial goals. While we can't tell you how to manage your investment portfolio during a volatile market, we are issuing this Investor Alert to give you the tools to make an informed decision. Before you make any decision, consider these areas of importance:

1. Draw A Personal Financial Roadmap.

Before you make any investing decision, sit down and take an honest look at your entire financial situation especially if you've never made a financial plan before. The first step to successful investing is figuring out your goals and risk tolerance either on your own or with the help of a financial professional. There is no guarantee that you'll make money from your investments. But if you get the facts about saving and investing and follow through with an intelligent plan, you should be able to gain financial security over the years and enjoy the benefits of managing your money.

2. Evaluate Your Comfort Zone In Taking On Risk.

All investments involve some degree of risk. If you intend to purchase securities - such as stocks, bonds, or mutual funds - you must understand before you invest that you could lose some or all of your money. Unlike deposits at FDIC-insured banks and NCUA-insured credit unions, the money you invest in securities typically is not federally insured. You could lose your principal, which is the amount you've invested.

"That's true even if you purchase your investments through a bank".

The reward for taking on risk is the potential for a greater investment return. If you have a financial goal with a long time horizon, you are likely to make more money by carefully investing in asset categories with greater risk, like stocks or bonds, rather than restricting your investments to assets with less risk, like cash equivalents. On the other hand, investing solely in cash investments may be appropriate for short-term financial goals. The principal concern for individuals investing in cash equivalents is inflation risk, which is the risk that inflation will outpace and erode returns over time.

Federally Insured Deposits at Banks and Credit Unions -- If you're not sure if your deposits are backed by the full faith and credit of the U.S. government, it's easy to find out.

3. Consider An Appropriate Mix Of Investments.

By including asset categories with investment returns that move up and down under different market conditions within a portfolio, an investor can help protect against significant losses. Historically, the returns of the three major asset categories stocks, bonds, and cash have not moved up and down at the same time. Market conditions that cause one asset category to do well often cause another asset category to have average or poor returns. By investing in more than one asset category, you'll reduce the risk that you'll lose money and your portfolio's overall investment returns will have a smoother ride. If one asset category's investment return falls, you'll be in a position to counteract your losses in that asset category with better investment returns in another asset category.

Also, asset allocation is important because it has a major impact on whether you will meet your financial goal. If you don't include enough risk in your portfolio, your investments may not earn a large enough return to meet your goal. For example, if you are saving for a long-term goal, such as retirement or college, most financial experts agree that you will likely need to include at least some stock or stock mutual funds in your portfolio.

Lifecycle Funds: To accommodate investors who prefer to use one investment to save for a particular investment goal, such as retirement, some mutual fund companies have begun offering a product known as a "lifecycle fund." A lifecycle fund is a diversified mutual fund that automatically shifts towards a more conservative mix of investments as it approaches a particular year in the future, known as its "target date." A lifecycle fund investor picks a fund with the right target date based on his or her particular investment goal. The managers of the fund then make all decisions about asset allocation, diversification, and rebalancing. It's easy to identify a lifecycle fund because its name will likely refer to its target date.

4. Be Careful If Investing Heavily In Shares Of Employer's Stock Or Any Individual Stock.

One of the most important ways to lessen the risks of investing is to diversify your investments. It's common sense: don't put all your eggs in one basket. By picking the right group of investments within an asset category, you may be able to limit your losses and reduce the fluctuations of investment returns without sacrificing too much potential gain.

You'll be exposed to significant investment risk if you invest heavily in shares of your employer's stock or any individual stock. If that stock does poorly or the company goes bankrupt, you'll probably lose a lot of money (and perhaps your job).

5. Create And Maintain An Emergency Fund.

Most smart investors put enough money in a savings product to cover an emergency, like sudden unemployment. Some make sure they have up to six months of their income in savings so that they know it will be there for them when they need it.

6. Pay Off High-Interest Credit Card Debt.

There is no investment strategy anywhere that pays off as well as, or with less risk than, merely paying off all high-interest debt you may have. If you owe money on high-interest credit cards, the wisest thing you can do under any market conditions is to pay off the balance in full as quickly as possible.

7. Consider Dollar-Cost Averaging.

Through the investment strategy known as "dollar-cost averaging," you can protect yourself from the risk of investing all of your money at the wrong time by following a consistent pattern of adding new money to your investment over a long period. By making regular investments with the same amount of money each time, you will buy more of an investment when its price is low and less of the investment when its price is high. Individuals that typically make a lump-sum contribution to an individual retirement account either at the end of the calendar year or in early April may want to consider "dollar cost averaging" as an investment strategy, especially in a volatile market.

8. Take Advantage Of "Free Money" From The Employer.

In many employer-sponsored retirement plans, the employer will match some or all of your contributions. If your employer offers a retirement plan and you do not contribute enough to get your employer's maximum match, you are passing up "free money" for your retirement savings.

9. Consider Rebalancing The Portfolio Occasionally.

Rebalancing is bringing your portfolio back to your original asset allocation mix. By rebalancing, you'll ensure that your portfolio does not overemphasize one or more asset categories, and you'll return your portfolio to a comfortable level of risk.

Stick With Your Plan: Buy Low, Sell High, Shifting money away from an asset category when it is doing well in favor of an asset category that is doing poorly may not be easy, but it can be a wise move. By cutting back on the current "winners" and adding more of the current so-called "losers," rebalancing forces you to buy low and sell high.

You can rebalance your portfolio based either on the calendar or on your investments. Many financial experts recommend that investors rebalance their portfolios on a regular time interval, such as every six or twelve months. The advantage of this method is that the calendar is a reminder of when you should consider rebalancing. Others recommend rebalancing only when the relative weight of an asset class increases or decreases more than a certain percentage that you've identified in advance. The advantage of this method is that your investments tell you when to rebalance.

In either case, rebalancing tends to work best when done on a relatively infrequent basis.

10. Avoid Circumstances That Can Lead To Fraud.

Scam artists read the headlines, too. Often, they'll use a highly publicized news item to lure potential investors and make their "opportunity" sound more legitimate. The SEC recommends that you ask questions and check out the answers with an unbiased source before you invest. Always take your time and talk to trusted friends and family members before investing.

5 Essential Tips For Investing In Stocks

These five stock tips will help you find winners, manage emotions, and keep perspective during tumultuous times.

5 Stock Market Investment Tips

- Check your emotions at the door.
- Pick companies, not stocks.
- Plan ahead for panicky times.
- Build up your stock positions with a minimum of risk.

- ❖ Avoid trading overactivity.

1. Check Your Emotions At The Door

"Success in investing doesn't correlate with IQ: what you need is the temperament to control the urges that get other people into trouble in investing." That's wisdom from Warren Buffett, chairman of Berkshire Hathaway, and an oft-quoted investing sage and role model for investors seeking long-term, market-beating, wealth-building returns.

Buffett is referring to investors who let their heads, not their guts, drive their investing decisions. Trading overactivity triggered by emotions is one of the most common ways investors hurt their portfolio returns. All the stock market tips that follow can help investors cultivate the temperament required for long-term success.

2. Pick Companies, Not Ticker Symbols

It's easy to forget that behind the alphabet soup of stock quotes crawling along the bottom of every CNBC broadcast is an actual business. But don't let stock picking become an abstract concept. Remember: Buying a share of a company's stock makes you a part-owner of that business.

Remember: Buying a share of a company's stock makes you a part-owner of that business.

You'll come across an overwhelming amount of information as you screen potential business partners. But it's easier to home in on the right stuff when wearing a "business buyer" hat. You want to know how this company operates, its place in the overall industry, its competitors, its long-term prospects, and whether it brings something new to the portfolio of businesses you already own.

3. Plan Ahead For Panicky Times

All investors are sometimes tempted to change their relationship statuses with their stocks. But making heat-of-the-moment decisions can lead to the classic investing gaffe: buying high and selling low. Write down what makes every stock in your portfolio worthy of a commitment and, while your head is clear, the circumstances that would justify a breakup. For example:

Why I'm Buying: Spell out what you find attractive about the company and the opportunity you see for the future. What are your expectations? What metrics matter most and what milestones will you use to judge the company's progress? Catalog the potential pitfalls and mark which ones would be game-changers and which would be signs of a temporary setback.

What Would Make Me Sell: Sometimes there are good reasons to split up. For this part of your journal, compose an investing prenup that spells out what would drive you to sell the stock. We're not talking about stock price movement, especially not short term, but fundamental changes to the business that affect its ability to grow over the long term. Some examples: The company loses a major customer, the CEO's successor starts taking the business in a different direction, a major viable competitor emerges, or your investing thesis doesn't pan out after a reasonable period.

4. Build Up Positions Gradually

Time, not timing, is an investor's superpower. The most successful investors buy stocks because they expect to be rewarded via share price appreciation, dividends, etc. over the years or even decades. That means you can take your time in buying, too. Here are three buying strategies that reduce your exposure to price volatility:

Dollar-Cost Average: This sounds complicated, but it's not. Dollar-cost averaging means investing a set amount of money at regular intervals, such as once per week or month. That set amount buys more shares when the stock price goes down and fewer shares when it rises, but overall, it evens out the average price you pay. Some online brokerage firms let investors set up an automated investing schedule.

Buy In Thirds: Like dollar-cost averaging, "buying in thirds" helps you avoid the morale-crushing experience of bumpy results right out of the gate. Divide the amount you want to invest by three and then, as the name implies, pick three separate points to buy shares. These can be at regular intervals (e.g., monthly or quarterly) or based on performance or company events. For example, you might buy shares before a product is released and put the next third of your money into play if it's a hit or divert the remaining money elsewhere if it's not.

Buy "The Basket": Can't decide which of the companies in a particular industry will be the long-term winner? Buy 'em all! Buying a basket of stocks takes the pressure off picking "the one." Having a stake in all the players that pass muster in your analysis means you won't miss out if one takes off, and you can use gains from that winner to offset any losses. This strategy will also help you identify which company is "the one" so you can double down on your position if desired.

5. Avoid Trading Overactivity

Checking in on your stocks once per quarte such as when you receive quarterly reports is plenty. But it's hard not to keep a constant eye on the scoreboard. This can lead to overreacting to short-term events, focusing on share price instead of company value, and feeling like you need to do something when no action is warranted.

When one of your stocks experiences a sharp price movement, find out what triggered the event. Is your stock the victim of collateral damage from the market responding to an unrelated event? Has something changed in the underlying business of the company? Is it something that meaningfully affects your long-term outlook?

Chapter 3 - Investing In Stock Markets

How To Start Investing In Stocks: A Beginner's Guide

Investing is a way to set aside money while you are busy with life and have that money work for you so that you can fully reap the rewards of your labor in the future. Investing is a means to a happier ending. Legendary investor Warren Buffett defines investing as "...the process of laying out money now to receive more money in the future."1 The goal of investing is to put your money to work in one or more types of investment vehicles in the hopes of growing your money over time. Let's say that you have $1,000 set aside, and you're ready to enter the world of investing. Or maybe you only have $10 extra a week, and you'd like to get into investing. In this article, we'll walk you through getting started as an investor and show you how to maximize your returns while minimizing your costs.

Facts: Investing is defined as the act of committing money or capital to an endeavor with the expectation of obtaining an additional income or profit. Unlike consuming, investing earmarks money for the future, hoping that it will grow over time. Investing, however, also comes with the risk of losses. Investing in the stock market is the most common way for beginners to gain investment experience.

What Kind Of Investor Are You?

Before you commit your money, you need to answer the question, what kind of investor am I? When opening a brokerage account, an online broker like Charles Schwab or Fidelity will ask you about your investment goals and how much risk you're willing to take on. Some investors want to take an active hand in managing their money's growth, and some prefer to "set it and forget it." More "traditional" online brokers, like the two mentioned above, allow you to invest in stocks, bonds, exchange-traded funds (ETFs), index funds, and mutual funds.

Why Invest In Stocks

Stocks are but one of many possible ways to invest your hard-earned money. Why choose stocks instead of other options, such as bonds, rare coins, or antique sports cars? Quite simply, the reason that savvy investors invest in stocks is that they provide the highest potential returns. And over the long term, no other type of investment tends to perform better.

On the downside, stocks tend to be the most volatile investments. This means that the value of stocks can drop in the short term. Sometimes stock prices may even fall for a protracted period. For instance, the 10-year return for the S&P 500 was slightly negative as recently as late 2010, largely due to the 2008 financial crisis and the early 2000s tech bubble bursting. Bad luck or bad timing can easily sink your returns, but you can minimize this by taking a long-term investing approach.

There's also no guarantee you will realize any sort of positive return. If you have the misfortune of consistently picking stocks that decline in value, you can lose money, even over the long term!

Of course, we think that by educating yourself and using the knowledge in this Investing Classroom, you can make the risk acceptable relative to your expected reward. We will help you pick the right businesses to own and help you spot the ones to avoid. Again, this effort is well worth it, because, over the long haul, your money can work harder for you in equities than in just about any other investment.

How To Invest In Stocks: A 10-Step Guide To Stock Trading

If you've never invested in the stock market before, it can be an intimidating process. Stocks are not like savings accounts, money market funds, or certificates of deposit, in that their principal value can both rise and fall. If you don't have sufficient knowledge of investing or emotional control you can lose most or even all of your investment capital. That's why learning the basics of how to invest in stocks is so important.

If you want to buy stocks, you'll need an online broker. We recommend using E*TRADE or Ally Invest to buy and sell stocks. Still, you'll need to know a lot more if you want to jumpstart your stock-market investing journey. If you want to get into investing but don't feel like an expert, read on.

Learn To Invest In Stocks In 10 Steps

- Step 1. Determine Your Goals
- Step 2. Put Some Money to the Side
- Step 3. Open a Retirement Account
- Step 4. Start Investing with a Low-Cost Online Service
- Step 5. Begin with Mutual Funds or Exchange Traded Funds (ETFs)
- Step 6. Stay with Index Funds
- Step 7. Use Dollar-Cost Averaging
- Step 8. Get Some Investment Education
- Step 9. Invest in Individual Stocks Gradually
- Step 10. Don't Forget to Diversify!

Step 1. Determine Your Goals

Before you get into investing of any kind, you first have to make sure that your overall financial situation is in a position to accommodate the new activity. Your financial baggage includes everything from income to debt, to your household budget. You can organize your finances for free with our favorite budgeting app, Personal Capital.

Specific Considerations Include:

1. **Employment:** Make sure that both your job and your income are secure enough to allow you to begin investing.

2. **Debt:** If you have a significant amount of outstanding credit, you may want to pay some debt down before you begin investing; you should never invest money you can't afford to lose, and that's the position you'll be in if you have too much debt.
3. **Family situation:** If you just welcomed a baby into the world, you may need all of your available income to help with the new arrival; family situations should be stable before you begin investing.
4. **Your household budget:** You should have some room in your budget to direct cash into your investment ventures.

It's also helpful to consider your goals and ask yourself why you want to start investing:'

- ❖ Are these investment accounts for your retirement?
- ❖ Is this money for a shorter-term goal, more like 5–6 years away?
- ❖ Will anyone else have access to this money?

Using these three questions as the starting point of your investing will help shape the decisions you need to make next. And they require no knowledge of the stock market! These are highly personal questions that each investor needs to answer for themselves. There's no right answer, just the correct answer for your life and goals. Investing makes the most sense for the longer term. You generally don't want to invest money that you need in fewer than five years, as there is a risk of losing that money in a downturn.

Step 2. Put Some Money To The Side

Before you put any of your money at risk, you should first have some put away that will not be subject to any risk whatsoever. A cash reserve equal to at least three months' living expenses should be the minimum, and it should sit in nothing riskier then certificates of deposit or money market accounts.

The purpose of the cash reserve is twofold:

- Act as an emergency fund in the event of a temporary income disruption or other financial emergencies
- Keep you from panicking should your risk type investments take a sudden dive.
- Keep Your Money Safe with a Betterment Cash Account

Step 3. Open A Retirement Account

Once you have a well-stocked emergency fund set up, the best place to begin investing is in a retirement account. This retirement account can be a 401(k) plan (or its equivalent) through your employer, or an Individual Retirement Account (IRA) if there is no employer plan.

Retirement accounts are an excellent start because they represent long-term investing. Besides, they are tax-sheltered and can produce immediate tax savings and are typically funded through payroll deductions. You can think of them as patient capital, where you have decades to accumulate and grow your money.

One of the best aspects of a retirement account is that you can build up money in the plan without actually investing any money until you're ready to do so. You can keep it all in a money market account within the plan until you feel comfortable adding stocks and funds to the plan.

There are a lot of retirement investment accounts, and you may or may not have access to all of them. Here's a quick rundown of the most common retirement accounts you might come across:

- 401(k)
- 403(b)
- Roth IRA
- Traditional IRA
- SEP IRA

There are a lot of differences between these accounts. And you may not be able to open and fund all of them.

Employer-Sponsored Retirement Accounts

Generally, your first step would be to find out if your job offers a workplace-sponsored retirement account like a 401(k) or a 403(b). Individual companies may have limits on what you can invest in or how long you have to work at the company before you can begin contributing to the plan.

These accounts may also come with an employer match, which is when an employer contributes the same amount of money or a percentage of what you add to the account. It's free money for your investments!, Reach out to your HR department and see what retirement plans are offered. Then get the ball rolling on signing up for one. And for our brand new investors, feel free to ask HR a lot of questions about how the plan works. You want to understand as much as you can about your plan when you begin to invest money in it.

Individual Retirement Accounts (IRAs)

After you sign up for a workplace retirement plan, you have the option of opening an IRA for yourself. IRA stands for "individual retirement account." Anyone over the age of 18 with income can open one for themselves. IRAs are not generally tied to an employer, making them appealing to freelancers and part-time employees. There are several options for IRAs, and they each have different details. There are income limits for a Roth IRA, for example. Do some research on which account is best for you before you open any of them. You can start with our article that compares various retirement accounts.

Step 4. Start Investing With A Low-Cost Online Service

Once you have a retirement account up and running, it's time to start investing for your non-retirement investing needs.

Use A Robo Advisor

If you're not the type of person who wants to DIY their investing accounts, you might be happy using a Robo advisor. Robo advisors use algorithms to help create the ideal portfolio mix for your needs and risk tolerance, usually by investing in exchange-traded funds (ETFs). Usually, you don't get to pick and choose individual stocks or funds the Robo advisor does it all for you. You can truly "set it and forget it."

Betterment is an excellent robot advisor choice for new investors because:

- There's no initial minimum deposit requirement
- You can build the fund with periodic contributions as low as $100 per month
- Its fees are among the lowest in the industry

One disadvantage of a Robo advisor such as Betterment is that investing in the account is limited. You buy into either a basket of stock-related ETFs or a basket of bond ETFs. However, this is not a problem when you're first starting.

Still, when you're ready to spread your capital around the investment universe and particularly into individual stocks, you'll need to look for a full-service broker to meet your needs. If you want to find a financial advisor who can not only help you invest, but also help you plan for the future, you can use a service like Paladin Registry. This service helps you find a registered advisor who is legally required to act in your best interest.

Use An Online Stock Broker

As opposed to hands-off Robo advisors, online stock brokers let you do the trading yourself. That means researching, choosing, buying and selling stocks, options, funds, etc., on your own. A great stockbroker choice for beginners is Merrill Edge. As a subsidiary of Bank of America, you can simplify your finances by having your bank and investing account in one place. Like other stockbrokers, stock trades are commission-free, although you will have to pay a small fee for more advanced trades like options and mutual funds. Merrill Edge offers a lot of account options, including IRAs, 529s, and taxable investment accounts.

Step 5. Begin With Mutual Funds Or Exchange Traded Funds (Etfs)

When you begin investing, you'll be far better off with mutual funds and ETFs than plunging right into stocks. Funds are professionally managed, and this will remove the burden of stock selection from your plate. All you need to do is:

- ❖ Open an account with one of the many commission-free ETF trading apps available (such as Public.com)
- ❖ Determine how much money you want to put into a given fund or group of funds, and then you're free to get on with the rest of your life.
- ❖ One of the advantages of mutual funds is that you also don't have to worry about diversification. Since each fund holds numerous stocks, diversification will already be built into the fund.

Step 6. Stay With Index Funds

To make mutual fund investing even more hassle-free, stick with index funds. For example, index funds that track the Standard & Poor's 500 indexes are invested in the broad market, so your investment performance will track that index precisely. While you'll never outperform the market in an index fund, you'll never under-perform it either. As a new investor, this is as it should be. Wealthfront is an excellent robot advisor to handle both your index funds and ETFs.

Step 7. Use Dollar-Cost Averaging

Dollar-cost averaging is the process of buying into your investment positions gradually, rather than all at once. For example, rather than investing $5,000 in a single index fund, you can make periodic contributions of, say, $100 per month into the fund. By doing this, you remove the possibility of buying at the top of the market. Instead, you're buying into the fund at all different times and continuously. This also eliminates the "when" question, as in when to invest in a given security or fund. Even better for you, dollar-cost averaging works beautifully with payroll contributions and is a natural fit with mutual funds and ETFs. You can set up automatic investments through Robo advisor M1 Finance.

Step 8. Get Some Investment Education

We could have made this step number three, with the intention that you have some understanding of investing before doing anything at all. Fortunately, mutual funds and ETFs with the help of index funds and dollar-cost averaging remove that necessity. You can begin investing immediately, even if you're a novice. But if you want to move beyond funds, payroll contributions, and dollar-cost averaging and into holding individual stocks

"You'll need to learn all that you can about investing before you do".

While you are accumulating money for investments and piling them into mutual funds and ETFs, you should use this time to educate yourself about the game of investing. Read books, listen to CDs, read The Wall Street Journal, take a course or two at a brokerage firm or even a community college, join investment forums, and regularly visit investment websites, like InvestorJunkie.com.

Vanguard is another excellent resource and possible investment platform to utilize. They currently offer a Personal Advisory Service for anyone that can invest at least $50,000 to start. The fee for the service is only 0.3% and you'll be provided all of the 1 on 1 support you can imagine.

Step 9. Invest In Individual Stocks Gradually

When you finally feel comfortable enough to begin investing in stocks, be sure that you do it gradually. You generally don't have the dollar-cost averaging feature when investing in individual stocks, so you'll have to develop your method for doing this on a gradual basis. Since you will already have significant positions in mutual funds and ETFs, you can begin investing in stocks one at a time as you work toward building a portfolio. The fund positions should prevent overexposure to a single stock, as long as you make sure that your position in the stock represents only a small minority of your total portfolio (generally 10% or less). You can buy individual stocks using E*TRADE, for example.

Never overload in a single stock. When you are starting, take a minimal position in one stock generally 100 shares to take advantage of the best pricing and then move into another stock. Repeat the process until you have several stock positions in your portfolio, in addition to your mutual funds and ETFs.

Step 10. Don't Forget To Diversify!

If you have set up a cash reserve, a retirement plan, and an investment account, and have begun stocking the retirement and investment accounts with mutual funds and ETFs, you've already taken a huge step toward diversifying your portfolio. Adding individual stocks will further diversify your cash and fund holdings. But while you are building your portfolio, you'll also need to spread your capital out among various equity sectors.

For example, depending on your age and risk tolerance, you might want to have some of your portfolio invested in bonds, growth and income funds, and international funds. You may also want to consider high dividend stocks among your stock holdings. Income earning securities tend to be less volatile than pure growth stocks, particularly in bear markets. You'll want to develop a balance between your growth assets and your income- or growth and income-holdings. A good management firm such as Fisher Investments can help you maintain the proper diversification and allocation of your investment account.

Why You Should Start Investing... Now

Numbers don't lie, and the truth of the matter is this: The earlier you start investing, the better off you're likely to be. The longer you keep your money invested, the more time it has to grow. Earlier investors have a better chance of seeing a more significant overall return on their investments by the time they withdraw money from the market. Take these steps, and you'll have the basic foundation to help you in getting started with stock trading. Just remember that, as we noted in our how to invest guide, investing is a process, not a destination, so you need to be learning and experimenting on an ongoing basis.

Chapter 4 - Common Approaches To Investing

Investment Strategies

Investment strategies are the game plan for your portfolio. Use the one that's right for you and significantly increase your chances of success. People extensively plan for their workday, a vacation, college financing, golf matches, buying a car, but they often forget about the most plan-required task of them all: investing. Investing your money without an investment strategy is like a football team going into a game without a playbook, although they are not required, they significantly improve your chances of winning. Creating an investment strategy is a seamless, number two-step, after learning the ins and out's of stock quotes and how to buy them.

The Importance Of Defining Your Investment Strategy

Having an investment strategy is like having an instruction booklet guiding you through the investment process. It will help you discard many potential investments that may perform poorly over time or that are not right for the investment goals you are looking to achieve. The best thing about investing strategies is that they're flexible. If you choose one and it doesn't suit your risk tolerance or schedule, you can certainly make changes. But be forewarned: doing so can be expensive. Every purchase carries a fee. More importantly, selling assets can create a realized capital gain. These gains are taxable and therefore, expensive.

Here, we look at common investing strategies that suit most investors. By taking the time to understand the characteristics of each, you will be in a better position to choose one that's right for you over the long-term without the need to incur the expense of changing course.

There are many different trading approaches available to investors. The selection of the trading approaches should take into account the level of risk the investor is willing to take on, the investment time horizon, and the life circumstances of the investors. For instance, an investor who is retired will need income to fund their living expenses whereas a young investor who is still working can engage in more risk as retirement is still a long way off. See below six different investment approaches.

1. Value Investing

The strategy of value investing is to find stocks that are under-priced and good value. Warren Buffet is a fan of this investment strategy. This strategy requires a detailed fundamental analysis of the company. Value investors look at stocks that have a market price (stock price) which is lower than the intrinsic value of the company. Intrinsic value is defined as the discounted value of the cash that can be taken out of a business during its remaining life. This value is an estimate which is dependant on interest rate movements or forecasted cash flow. A stock price is more than the intrinsic value when there is strong demand, driving the prices up. This strategy is more suited to the long term investor as these value stocks may take a long time before their stock prices rise. Stocks with lower P/E ratios will be more favorable under value investing. A cheaper stock does not always mean a profitable stock as the business may have serious issues. Hence research on the company is necessary when evaluating a value stock.

2. Income Investing

This strategy involves buying securities that generate income for the investor. Stocks that have a high dividend yield are selected as investors are looking for income-producing stocks. Bond proxies have been popular in income investing. Such stocks include real estate trusts (REITs) and listed infrastructure. These are defensive stocks but have a higher dividend yield compared to the bond market. Stocks that have a high dividend rate may not have as much capital growth appreciation as a stock that pays no dividends. The reason is that companies that forgo dividend payouts reinvest those earnings into the business for expansion. The strategy of finding companies that pay high dividends is appropriate for investors who are living off their investment portfolios to fund their living expenses. This strategy is suited to the conservative investor as companies who can pay large dividends tend to be established stable companies.

3. Growth Investing

This strategy involves selecting companies that have the potential to grow rapidly in the future. These stocks may be expensive in comparison to what the company is earning currently as the market has already priced in future growth in these companies. Growth companies reinvest their earnings to grow the business further and hence may not pay a dividend at all. This strategy is more suited to the risk of seeking investors as these stocks are more volatile than average. Growth stocks have the possibility of large capital growth gains if stocks are selected well. It is suited to the investor who does not need income from their investment portfolio and is willing to sacrifice income for capital growth.

4. Small-Cap Investing

Another strategy for the risk-seeking investor in small-cap investing. This strategy is suited to an investor who does not need access to their capital for a while. A small-cap stock is defined as a company with a market capitalization between $300million and $2billion. Small-cap stocks have historically performed well when there are interest rates rise and the economy is strong. However large-cap stocks perform better during periods of recessions. These stocks are chosen for their potential for future growth, but with a small market cap, their volatility is higher. Unlike growth investing, small-cap stocks tend to be priced cheaply as the business is still in its infancy. The reason why small-cap stocks have a higher propensity for capital growth than stocks in the top 20 is that they are still in the growth phase of the business cycle. It's easier for a company with a market cap of 300m to double in size than stock in the top 20.

5. Active Investing

This strategy involves frequent buying and selling of stocks to take advantage of stock volatility and stock mispricing. An active investor typically holds positions within hours, days, or months. Technical analysis is more of a focus than fundamental analysis as the investor is not investing in the stock for the long-term frame. Active investors change stocks in the portfolio depending on the market, economic, and company conditions. These investors will cut stocks that aren't performing or are stagnate rather than hold the stock long term anticipating the stock will appreciate. The purpose of active investing is to beat the market and outperform the index.

6. Passive Investing

Passive investors believe the market is priced efficiently and they hold shares that track an index. The is strategy is to match the returns of the market. These investors buy and hold securities for the long term and there less frequent trading. Stocks are only sold and brought when companies leave and enter the indices. If there are large share price drops, passive investors hold onto the stock in the hope that over time it will recover. The returns with passive investing tend me to be smaller than active investing as it seeks to track the index and not beat it. However, transaction costs are lower due to less trading.

How To Choose An Investing Strategy That's Right For You

Setting up your investment strategy is like buying a new car before you look at the different models, you need to figure out what style suits you best. And just like cars, there are many styles to choose from when creating an investment strategy. When choosing the right investing strategy, some questions need to be answered first. What is your investment horizon? What returns are you seeking to achieve? What amount of risk are you able to tolerate? What are the funds in this investment to be used for? Answering these questions will ultimately also help in building your portfolio.

Determining what will be your breakdown between cash, fixed-income securities and stocks is a good start towards creating your investment strategy. The breakdown of your asset allocation ultimately depends on your risk tolerance. A conservative investor may prefer to hold 80% of his portfolio in fixed-income and 20% in stocks. The reverse would be true for an aggressive investor, while a balanced investor will follow a 50-50 split.

In terms of specific investment strategies within your asset allocation, if you are a high-risk investor with a long investment horizon, you may want to include small-cap and growth investing in your portfolio. If you have a moderate risk tolerance and a shorter investment horizon, you may be more suitable for value and income investing. If you have a low-risk tolerance and short investment horizon, you may want to focus solely on income investing. For those looking for companies that aim to not harm, you can add socially responsible assets to your portfolio with relative ease. It is also important to adapt to the investment strategy you are most comfortable with. Someone with a knack for choosing growth stocks may make that strategy the priority in their portfolio.

Chapter 5 - How To Use Fundamental Analysis When Investing

What Is Fundamental Analysis?

In accounting and finance, fundamental analysis is a method of assessing the intrinsic value of a security by analyzing various macroeconomic and microeconomic factors. The ultimate goal of fundamental analysis is to quantify the intrinsic value of a security. Its intrinsic value can then be compared to its current market price to help with investment decisions. Unlike technical analysis that concentrates on forecasting a security's price movements, the fundamental analysis aims to determine the "correct price" (true value) of security. By knowing the right price, an investor can make an informed investment decision. Security can be overvalued, undervalued, or fairly valued.

Understanding Fundamental Analysis

All stock analysis tries to determine whether a security is correctly valued within the broader market. Fundamental analysis is usually done from a macro to micro perspective to identify securities that are not correctly priced by the market. Analysts typically study, in order, the overall state of the economy and then the strength of the specific industry before concentrating on individual company performance to arrive at a fair market value for the stock. Fundamental analysis uses public data to evaluate the value of a stock or any other type of security. For example, an investor can perform fundamental analysis on a bond's value by looking at economic factors such as interest rates and the overall state of the economy, then studying information about the bond issuer, such as potential changes in its credit rating.

For stocks, the fundamental analysis uses revenues, earnings, future growth, return on equity, profit margins and other data to determine a company's underlying value and potential for future growth. Fundamental analysis is used most often for stocks, but it is useful for evaluating any security, from a bond to a derivative. If you consider the fundamentals, from the broader economy to the company details, you are doing fundamental analysis.

Investing And Fundamental Analysis

An analyst uses works to create a model for determining the estimated value of a company's share price based on publicly available data. This value is only an estimate, the analyst's educated opinion, of what the company's share price should be worth compared to the current trading market price. Some analysts may refer to their estimated price as the company's intrinsic value.

If an analyst calculates that the stock's value should be significantly higher than the stock's current market price, they may publish a buy or overweight rating for the stock. This acts as a recommendation to investors who follow that analyst. If the analyst calculates a lower intrinsic value than the current market price, the stock is considered overvalued and a sell or underweight recommendation is issued.

Investors who follow these recommendations will expect that they can buy stocks with favorable recommendations because such stocks should have a higher probability of rising over time. Likewise, stocks with unfavorable ratings are expected to have a higher probability of falling in price. Such stocks are candidates for being removed from existing portfolios or added as "short positions. This method of stock analysis is considered to be the opposite of technical analysis, which forecasts the direction of prices through an analysis of historical market data such as price and volume.

Quantitative And Qualitative Fundamental Analysis

The problem with defining the word fundamentals is that it can cover anything related to the economic well-being of a company. They include numbers like revenue and profit, but they can also include anything from a company's market share to the quality of its management. The various fundamental factors can be grouped into two categories: quantitative and qualitative. The financial meaning of these terms isn't much different from their standard definitions. Here is how a dictionary defines the terms:

- Quantitative – capable of being measured or expressed in numerical terms.
- Qualitative – related to or based on the quality or character of something, often as opposed to its size or quantity.

In this context, quantitative fundamentals are hard numbers. They are the measurable characteristics of a business. That's why the biggest source of quantitative data is financial statements. Revenue, profit, assets, and more can be measured with great precision. The qualitative fundamentals are less tangible. They might include the quality of a company's key executives, brand-name recognition, patents, and proprietary technology. Neither qualitative nor quantitative analysis is inherently better. Many analysts consider them together.

Components Of Fundamental Analysis

Fundamental analysis consists of three main parts:

- Economic analysis
- Industry analysis
- Company analysis

Fundamental analysis is an extremely comprehensive approach that requires a deep knowledge of accounting, finance, and economics. For instance, fundamental analysis requires the ability to read financial statements, an understanding of macroeconomic factors, and knowledge of valuation techniques.

It primarily relies on public data, such as a company's historical earnings and profit margins, to project future growth.

Fundamental analysis is the process of evaluating security for creating forecasts about its future price. Fundamental analysis includes estimations based on many components related to stock, including:

- The global industry
- Company financial statements
- Company press releases
- News releases
- Domestic political conditions
- Trade agreements and external politics
- Competitor analysis

If some fundamental indicators of a company show data that has a bad impact, this is likely to negatively reflect the share price. On the other hand, if there's a positive data release, like an outstanding earnings report, for example, this can boost the stock price of the respective company. Here are some examples of key performance indices that are commonly used to analyze stocks fundamentally:

- Earnings per share (EPS)
- Price-to-earnings (P/E) ratio
- Price-to-book (P/B) ratio
- Return on equity

- Beta

Each of these key performance indices gives information that helps conduct a price analysis. You can buy the stock on the assumption that the price will increase if your analysis shows that the price of the stock is about to increase.

A Detailed Example Of Fundamental Analysis

There's no right way to do fundamental analysis, as stock trading is not as accurate as a math problem. The same information in different industries and different stocks will never mean the same thing. Here are a few of the most important fundamental indicators.

Earnings Per Share (EPS)

The earnings per share related to the portion of profit allocated to each of the company's shares. The EPS is an indication of the company's profitability. The higher the earnings per share, the better it is for the investor. A higher EPS is a symbol of a healthy company. At the same time, if the earnings per share are unusually high, this could mean one of the following things:

- Earnings can decrease and get back to normal.
- The price of the stock can increase to normalize the stock price compared to the earnings.

Price-To-Earnings Ratio (P/E Ratio)

The price-to-earnings (P/E) ratio shows the company payouts compared to the price of the stock. In other words, the P/E ratio shows whether a share of stock pays well compared to its price. We calculate the P/E ratio by dividing the price per share by the earnings per share.

For example, imagine that the price per share is $30 and the stock pays $2 earnings per share:

30 / 2 = 15

The lower the P/E ratio, the higher the earnings compared to the stock price.

At first sight, the lower the P/E ratio, the more attractive the stock. But if we think carefully we will realize that unusually low P/E ratio could show extra potential.

If the P/E ratio is too low, below 10 for example, this means that the price per share is low compared to the earnings. This might mean that the stock is undervalued in price and it can increase its price. The opposite is in force for the high P/E ratio.

Price-To-Book Ratio (P/B Ratio)

The price-to-book ratio is an indication that shows how much the stock worth compared to the book value of the company. If a company worth $10 million and has 500,000 shares outstanding, it will have a book value per share of:

10,000,000 / 500,000 = $20 book value per share

If the stock trades at $80 per share, then the price-to-book ratio is:

80 / 20 = 4 P/B ratio

The P/B ratio = price per share divided by the book value per share.

If the P/B ratio is more than 1, this means investors believe that the stock will grow at a faster pace, which is the reason why its price is higher than its book value. In some cases, you can even see P/B ratios of 100 and more. This could be a common parameter for the growth stocks.

Return On Equity (ROE)

The return on equity is a measurement that determines how efficient a company is when using the shareholders' equity. You calculate the ROE by dividing the shareholders' equity by the company's net income. If a company has generated $5 million this year and the shareholder equity is $50 million, this means the ROE is:

50,000,000 / 5,000,000 = 10%

Note that you should calculate the ROE result as a percentage.

The higher the ROE, the more efficient the company is. If a company generates a less than $5 million income this year (say $2 million) with the same shareholders' equity, this means it is less efficient:

50,000,000 / 2,000,000 = 4%

Here, the company has a lower ROE with the same shareholder's equity, meaning that it is less efficient.

Beta (β)

The beta gives information about the stock price's correlation to the industry it operates in. This happens by comparing the stock to a benchmark index. The beta usually varies between -1 and 1. Sometimes values can go much lower than -1 or much higher than 1.

Values above 0 mean that the stock correlates to the benchmark index. The higher the beta, the higher the correlation. But the higher beta also means that the volatility is higher as well, meaning that the risk of the asset increases.

Values below 0 mean that the stock is inversely correlated to the benchmark index. It won't be as a mirror image, but the ticks are likely to match. The lower the beta, the higher the inverse correlation. However, the lower the beta, the lower the volatility.

Fundamental Analysis Tools

Although earnings are important, they don't tell you much by themselves. On their own, earnings don't identify how the market values the stock. You'll need to incorporate more fundamental analysis tools to begin building a picture of how the stock is valued.

You can find most of these ratios completed for you on finance-related websites, but they aren't difficult to calculate on your own. If you want to wade in for yourself, keep in mind that some of the most popular tools of fundamental analysis focus on earnings, growth, and value in the market. These are some of the factors you'll want to identify and include:

Earnings Per Share (EPS): Neither earnings nor the number of shares can tell you much about a company on its own, but when you combine them, you get one of the most commonly used ratios for company analysis. EPS tells us how much of a company's profit is assigned to each share of stock. EPS is calculated as net income (after dividends on preferred stock) divided by the number of outstanding shares.

Price-To-Earnings Ratio (P/E): This ratio compares the current sales price of a company's stock to its per-share earnings.

Projected Earnings Growth (PEG): PEG anticipates the one-year earnings growth rate of the stock.

Price-To-Sales Ratio (P/S): The price-to-sales ratio values a company's stock price as compared to its revenues. It's also sometimes called the PSR, revenue multiple, or sales multiple.

Price-To-Book Ratio (P/B): This ratio, also known as the price-to-equity ratio, compares a stock's book value to its market value. You can arrive at it by dividing the stock's most recent closing price by last quarter's book value per share. Book value is the value of an asset, as it appears in the company's books. It's equal to the cost of each asset less cumulative depreciation.

Dividend Payout Ratio: This compares dividends paid out to the stockholders to the company's total net income. It accounts for retained earnings income that is not paid out, but rather, retained for potential growth.

Dividend Yield: This, too, is a ratio yearly dividends compared to share price. It's expressed as a percentage. Divide dividend payments per share in one year by the value of a share.

Return On Equity: Divide the company's net income by shareholders' equity to find its return on equity. You might also hear this expressed as the company's return on net worth.

Chapter 6 - How To Use Technical Analysis When Investing

What Is Technical Analysis?

Technical analysis is a process used to examine and predict the future prices of securities by looking at things like price movement, charts, trends, trading volume, and other factors. Unlike fundamental analysis, technical analysis focuses on trading signals to delineate good investments and trading opportunities by examining an investment's trends through its trading data and other statistical elements. As a general rule, technical analysis prizes the current or last price of a security as the best indicator of the future price of that security. Technical analysis relies heavily on financial charts, data, and statistics to uncover an investment's strengths or possible weaknesses and forecast trends to help analysts and investors decide if security is viable or not, and for what action.

Technical analysis is a tool, or method, used to predict the probable future price movement of security such as a stock or currency pair based on market data. The theory behind the validity of technical analysis is the notion that the collective actions buying and selling of all the participants in the market accurately reflect all relevant information about a traded security, and therefore, continually assign a fair market value to the security.

Types Of Technical Analysis

In general, there are two main approaches to examining stocks:

'Top-Down' Approach

When analysts are looking at stocks through a top-down approach, they generally analyze securities from a broader to more-specific viewpoint -- often going from looking at a major index like the S&P 500 to sector charts to specific weekly or hourly charts for certain stocks. Technical analysts continue to examine more and more specific charts to determine which stock looks like a good investment. When using the top-down approach, technical analysts examine a stock or security's moving averages in a more general-to-specific time frame, such as starting by looking at daily averages and then moving to examine hourly averages for a given stock's price movements.

For example, a trader might start by looking at how security is doing on a daily chart. If it's performing bullishly daily, the trader might then look at its hourly chart to find an optimum point of entry for the stock.

'Bottom-Up' Approach

By contrast, a bottom-up approach to technical analysis includes looking for potentially undervalued stocks and examining them on a more fundamental basis to find a point of entry where the stock looks like it's bottomed out. Technical analysts use the bottom-up approach to look at stocks that are disregarding the overall market's trend, then look for entry or exit points that would put them in the best position to make money on a given name.

Charting On Different Time Frames

Technical traders analyze price charts to attempt to predict price movement. The two primary variables for technical analysis are the time frames considered and the particular technical indicators that a trader chooses to utilize. The technical analysis time frames shown on charts range from one-minute to monthly, or even yearly, periods. Popular time frames that technical analysts most frequently examine include:

- 5-minute chart
- 15-minute chart
- Hourly chart
- 4-hour chart
- Daily chart

The time frame a trader selects to study is typically determined by that individual trader's trading style. Intra-day traders, traders who open and close trading positions within a single trading day, favor analyzing price movement on shorter time frame charts, such as the 5-minute or 15-minute charts. Long-term traders who hold market positions overnight and for long periods are more inclined to analyze markets using hourly, 4-hour, daily, or even weekly charts.

Price movement that occurs within 15 minutes may be very significant for an intraday trader who is looking for an opportunity to realize a profit from price fluctuations occurring during one trading day. However, that same price movement viewed on a daily or weekly chart may not be particularly significant or indicative of long-term trading purposes.

It's simple to illustrate this by viewing the same price action on different time frame charts. The following daily chart for silver shows price trading within the same range, from roughly $16 to $18.50, that it's been in for the past several months. A long-term silver investor might be inclined to look to buy silver based on the fact that the price is fairly near the low of that range.

Today the field of technical analysis builds on Dow's work. Professional analysts typically accept three general assumptions for the discipline:

1. The Market Discounts Everything

Technical analysts believe that everything from a company's fundamentals to broad market factors to market psychology is already priced into the stock. This point of view is congruent with the Efficient Markets Hypothesis (EMH) which assumes a similar conclusion about prices. The only thing remaining is the analysis of price movements, which technical analysts view as the product of supply and demand for a particular stock in the market.

2. Price Moves In Trends

Technical analysts expect that prices, even in random market movements, will exhibit trends regardless of the time frame being observed. In other words, a stock price is more likely to continue a past trend than move erratically. Most technical trading strategies are based on this assumption.

3. History Tends To Repeat Itself

Technical analysts believe that history tends to repeat itself. The repetitive nature of price movements is often attributed to market psychology, which tends to be very predictable based on emotions like fear or excitement. Technical analysis uses chart patterns to analyze these emotions and subsequent market movements to understand trends. While many forms of technical analysis have been used for more than 100 years, they are still believed to be relevant because they illustrate patterns in price movements that often repeat themselves.

How Technical Analysis Is Used

Technical analysis attempts to forecast the price movement of virtually any tradable instrument that is generally subject to forces of supply and demand, including stocks, bonds, futures, and currency pairs. Some view technical analysis as simply the study of supply and demand forces as reflected in the market price movements of a security. Technical analysis most commonly applies to price changes, but some analysts track numbers other than just prices, such as trading volume or open interest figures.

Across the industry, there are hundreds of patterns and signals that have been developed by researchers to support technical analysis trading. Technical analysts have also developed numerous types of trading systems to help them forecast and trade on price movements. Some indicators are focused primarily on identifying the current market trend, including support and resistance areas, while others are focused on determining the strength of a trend and the likelihood of its continuation. Commonly used technical indicators and charting patterns include trendlines, channels, moving averages, and momentum indicators.

In general, technical analysts look at the following broad types of indicators:

- Price trends
- Chart patterns
- Volume and momentum indicators
- Oscillators
- Moving averages
- Support and resistance levels

The Difference Between Technical Analysis And Fundamental Analysis

Fundamental analysis and technical analysis, the major schools of thought when it comes to approaching the markets, are at opposite ends of the spectrum. Both methods are used for researching and forecasting future trends in stock prices, and like any investment strategy or philosophy, both have their advocates and adversaries.

Fundamental analysis is a method of evaluating securities by attempting to measure the intrinsic value of a stock. Fundamental analysts study everything from the overall economy and industry conditions to the financial condition and management of companies. Earnings, expenses, assets, and liabilities are all important characteristics to fundamental analysts.

Technical analysis differs from fundamental analysis in that the stock's price and volume are the only inputs. The core assumption is that all known fundamentals are factored into price; thus, there is no need to pay close attention to them. Technical analysts do not attempt to measure a security's intrinsic value, but instead, use stock charts to identify patterns and trends that suggest what a stock will do in the future.

Limitations Of Technical Analysis

Some analysts and academic researchers expect that the EMH demonstrates why they shouldn't expect any actionable information to be contained in historical price and volume data. However, by the same reasoning, neither should business fundamentals provide any actionable information. These points of view are known as the weak form and semi-strong form of the EMH.

Another criticism of technical analysis is that history does not repeat itself exactly, so price pattern study is of dubious importance and can be ignored. Prices seem to be better modeled by assuming a random walk. A third criticism of technical analysis is that it works in some cases but only because it constitutes a self-fulfilling prophecy. For example, many technical traders will place a stop-loss order below the 200-day moving average of a certain company. If a large number of traders have done so and the stock reaches this price, there will be a large number of sell orders, which will push the stock down, confirming the movement traders anticipated.

Then, other traders will see the price decrease, and also sell their positions, reinforcing the strength of the trend. This short-term selling pressure can be considered self-fulfilling, but it will have little bearing on where the asset's price will be weeks or months from now. In sum, if enough people use the same signals, they could cause the movement foretold by the signal, but in the long run, this sole group of traders cannot drive price.

Choosing The Right Day-Trading Software

Computer applications have made it easy to automate trading, especially for short-term intensive activities like day trading, making the usage of trading software very popular. The debate continues over the profit potential that can be realistically derived from day-trading activities using online trading platforms, as brokerage fees and commissions are said to take away the major portion of available profit potential. It thus becomes very important to select the right day-trading software with a cost-benefit analysis, assessment of its applicability to individual trading needs and strategies, as well as the features and functions you need. Day trading is a time-bound trading activity where buy or sell positions are taken and closed on the same trading day to make profits in smaller price differentials on large order volumes by frequent buying and selling, usually on leverage.

What Is Day-Trading Software?

Day-trading software constitutes a computer program, usually provided by brokerage firms, to help clients carry out their day-trading activities in an efficient and timely manner. They often automate analysis and enter trades on their own that enable traders to reap profits that would be difficult to achieve by mere mortals. For example, a day trader may find it impossible to manually track two technical indicators (like 50- and 200-day moving averages) on three different stocks of his or her choice, but an automated day-trading software can easily do it and place trades once the set criteria are met. The features and functions available may differ from one software package to the next and may come in different versions. Apart from brokers, independent vendors also provide day-trading software, which tends to have more advanced features.

Day trading software is the general name for any software that helps you analyze, decide on, and make a trade. It may grant you access to all the technical analysis and indicator tools and resources you need. The best software may also identify trades and even automate or execute them in line with your strategy. Whether you're after trading software for beginners, or as an advanced trader, with more options than ever before, doing your research has never been so important. Firstly, you'll find out precisely how these software packages work. This page will then highlight what to look for from your broker's software offering, whilst breaking down forex software, stocks software, and others in detail. It will also touch upon software demo accounts, equipment, and the regional differences to be aware of.

Features And Functionality

The above is an example of arbitrage where trading opportunities are short-lived. A lot of these types of day-trading activities can be set up through day-trading software and thus it becomes extremely important to select the right one matching your needs. Some characteristics of good day-trading software:

Platform Independence: Unless a trader is running highly complex algorithms for day-trading requiring high-end dedicated computers, it is advisable to go with a web-based software offering. Benefits include connectivity from anywhere, no manual installations of upgrades, and no maintenance costs. However, if you are using highly complex algorithms that require advanced computing, then it is better to consider dedicated computer-based installable software, although that will be costly.

Your Specific Needs For Day Trading: Are you following a simple day-trading strategy of moving-average tracking on stocks, or are you looking to implement a complex delta-neutral trading strategy including options and stocks? Do you need a forex feed or are you trading on specific products like binary options? Trusting the claims on stockbrokers' website content is not enough to understand the offering. Ask for a trial version and thoroughly assess it during the initial phase. Alternatively, check the screen-by-screen tutorial (if available) from the stockbroker or vendor to clearly understand the right fit for your day-trading needs.

Additional Features: Day trading attempts to capitalize on short term price movements during the day. Such short-term price movements are in turn driven primarily by news and supply and demand (among other factors). Does your day-trading strategy require news, charts, Level 2 data, exclusive connectivity to particular markets (like OTC), specific data feeds, etc.? If so, are these included in the software or would the trader have to subscribe to them separately from other sources, thereby increasing the cost?

Analytical Features: Pay attention to the set of analytical features it offers. Here are a few of them:

Technical Indicators/Pattern Recognition: For traders who attempt to benefit from predicting the future price level and direction, a wealth of technical indicators is available. Once the trader finalizes the technical indicators to follow, they should ensure that the day-trading software supports the necessary automation for efficient processing of trades based on the desired technical indicator.

Arbitrage Opportunities Recognition: To benefit from the slight price difference of a dual-listed share on multiple markets, simultaneous buying (at a low price exchange) and selling (at a high price market) enables profit opportunities and is one of the commonly followed strategies using day-trading software. This requires a connection to both markets, the ability to check price differences as they occur, and execute trades promptly.

Mathematical Model-Based Strategies: Few automated trading strategies based on mathematical models exist like the delta-neutral trading strategy that allow trading on a combination of options and its underlying security, where trades are placed to offset positive and negative deltas so that the portfolio delta is maintained at zero. The day-trading software should have the in-built intelligence to assess the current holdings, verify available market prices, and execute trades for both equity and options as needed.

Trend Following Strategies: Another large set of strategies commonly implemented through day-trading software.

How Trading Software Works

Online day trading software can be broken down into four categories:

Data: Before you start trading for the day you need to know the prices of the stocks, futures, and/or currencies you want to trade. For stocks and futures, those prices will usually come from the exchange where they are traded. Forex, however, doesn't have a central exchange.

Charting: Smart traders will usually chart prices in charting software. Many vendors will also offer data feeds. These charting packages usually offer basic technical analysis indicators. Opt for a more advanced package and you can benefit from more indicators and the ability to backtest your strategies.

Trade Execution: With your data to hand and after analyzing it on a chart, at some point you'll want to enter a trade. For that, you'll need some sort of trade execution software, an electronic trading platform. A lot of software today will also allow you to develop your trading strategies with an application programming interface (API). They may also offer you automated trading capabilities specifically for day trading.

Broker Vs Independent Vendor: A lot of brokers will offer software directly linked to their in-house systems, but you can also use third-party applications through independent software vendors with brokers that support such integration. The benefit of third-party solutions is that they often have more advanced features and enable you to trade with several different brokers with one single interface.

Tools

Mac Or Windows?

When choosing your software you need something that works seamlessly with your desktop or laptop. Any crashes or technical issues could cost you serious profit. Fortunately, the day trader is no longer constrained to Windows computers, recent years have seen a surge in the popularity of day trading software for Mac.

MetaTrader4, for example, is the world's most popular trading platform. It's user-friendly, so combined with an easy to navigate Mac, it's ideal for both beginners and veterans. But whether you're looking for the best trading software for Mac or Windows, check reviews to ensure the technical tools, data feeds, portfolio trackers, backtesting capabilities and any other features you require won't run into compatibility hurdles. Also, make sure the initial trading software download is free. Reputable brokers shouldn't charge you for the installation privilege.

Mobile Day Trading Software

You can also get extremely useful mobile trading software, normally in the form of an app on iOS and Android. These aren't designed to replace desktop applications as they lack in the capabilities area. They are best used to supplement your normal trading software. Make sure when choosing your software that the mobile app comes free. A good app will provide succinct market updates, trends, and the usual stock price tickers. If the app overloads you with information that pushes you towards impulsive decisions, stay clear.

What To Look For

Brokers will often offer standard software, but if you want additional features that may be essential for your strategies then you may have to pay significantly more. To conduct a thorough software comparison before you start trading with your hard-earned capital.

Cost & Need

Does It Meet Your Needs?: There is no one size fits all. The different trading software will suit different people. Are you following a simple stocks strategy such as moving average tracking? Alternatively, do you want to employ a more complicated multi-conditional strategy? Will you need a direct forex feed? To make sure it caters to your needs get a free software download trial and practice day trading on it first.

Cost: How much does day trading software cost? It's all too easy to opt for the cheapest trading software. Whilst this may save you money in the short term, you may be sacrificing essential features your strategy requires. Adding these features later may cost you even more than if you'd invested in a comprehensive software to start with. Also, check to see if the software is available as part of the standard brokerage account, or does it come at an additional cost?

Technology

Execution Speed: Time is money and nowhere is that truer than in the day trading world. Ensure your software will allow you to enter and exit trades swiftly. Check reviews for any trade execution red flags. A few seconds could be the difference finishing being in the red or black at the end of the day.

Accessibility: Is it a web-based software offering? If so, you'll need just an internet connection to get online, plus you'll have zero installation, update, and maintenance costs. Web-based trading software is the best option for beginners. However, if you employ extremely complex algorithms, you may need a computer-based installable software. Bear in mind this will be a far more expensive route to go down.

Features: Day traders rely on short term price movements to turn a profit. What does your strategy need to monitor these price fluctuations? Will you need charts, particular data feeds, news sources, specific market access? If so, check whether these will be included as standard.

Analytics: Does your strategy depend on technical indicators and pattern recognition? Will the software recognize arbitrage opportunities? A comprehensive analysis software will provide you with all the analytical features you need in one user-friendly bundle.

Forex Trading Software

Which is the best forex trading software available in today's market? With hundreds to choose from, finding the right software for your needs isn't a straightforward decision. The first question to ask would be 'what information, resources and tools do you need to enhance your forex strategy?'

Below are some of the most popular currency trading software available:

Trading Platforms: These enable you to manually manage and execute forex trades.

Trading Signal Generators: These will provide you with recommended levels for which to enter and exit positions.

Technical Analysis Software: These will offer you charts of historical exchange rates, plus a wide range of technical indicators.

Automated Forex Trading Software: Once you've pre-programmed your rules and strategy, these programs will automatically execute trades on your behalf.

Stocks Trading Software

With today's volatile market trends, picking the right stock trading software is essential. It is often said that there are very few stocks worth trading each day. That means identifying them before they make their big move will be what separates the profitable traders and the rest. Before you purchase, always check the trading software reviews first. Also, look for the following capabilities from your software:

Market Scanning: The program should scan the market for potential opportunities and swiftly draw your attention to stocks of interest.

Charting Software: These will help you decipher market conditions, so look for software that keeps their charts user friendly, or even offers customizability options.

Portfolio Tracking: This will help you keep a close track of all previous trades, helping you to identify mistakes and hone your strategy.

Backtesting: The software should enable you to backtest your trading systems against historical data, giving you an idea of whether and how successful your strategy will be before you risk real capital.

Other Instruments & Markets

On top of the software for the instruments above, you can also get your hands on the following:

Commodity Trading Software: There's a rich supply of international trading software for the commodities markets. Plus, you can get your hands on some of the best free online trading and charting software around.

Bitcoin Day Trading Software: As the market is still growing, new options are popping up every month. You'll also find some of the best trading simulator software, that's probably free.

Emini Trading Software: Emini options continue to grow, so you can choose between generic systems or specialist Emini software. You'll also find lots of good scalping software options, with plenty of reviews on software forums.

Penny Stocks Software: There is healthy competition, so if you're looking at where to buy the best trading software for penny stocks, a quick Google will answer all your prayers in abundance. You can also find easy to use buy and sell signal software for penny stocks.

Software For NSE: You can find free trading software for Indian markets, or you can choose from the ever-growing options.

Software For Cryptocurrency: You can choose between robot, prediction software, or you can find plenty of manual options. You can also now get your hands on useful virtual money management software to keep your online wallet heavy.

Journal Software

Day trading journal software allows you to keep online logbooks. Why would you want that? Because they keep a detailed account of all your previous trades. They record the instrument, date, price, entry, and exit points. This allows you to not only fill in your tax returns with ease but also to analyze your recent trade performance. It could help you identify mistakes, enabling you to trade smarter in the future. This makes it some of the most important intraday trading software available.

Popular Software

Make sure when you compare software, you check the reviews first. Even the ones that proclaim to be one of the 'top 10-day trading software', can have some serious drawbacks. Also bear in mind, the easiest trading software won't necessarily be the best. If it's easy because it falls short of the essentials outlined above, your bottom line may suffer.

Having said that, consider the popular and well-regarded options below:

MetaTrader: Market-leading multi-functional trading platform. Integrated with many leading brokers.

TradingView: The leading charting package with a wealth of technical analysis tools and the ability to build and backtest strategies. It can also automate trades, and copy trade.

Linux Software: Considered some of the fastest real-time trading software around.

JSE Software: Considered one of the best futures day trading software available.

MCX Analysis Software: One of Tim Sykes highly recommended trading software systems.

TD Ameritrade: Some of the best live and virtual day trading software available, scoring particularly high in US reviews.

Etrade Software: Nifty trading software, that's fast, reliable, and used by traders of all levels.

Consors Software: This German software offers some of the best trading simulation software for free.

AlgoTrader: This is ideal if you're looking for customizable, open-source software to implement automated strategies.

NinjaTrader: Allows developers to build their integrated indicators.

ZuluTrade: Automate trades or copy trading signals or traders. Popular in the US.

E-Toro: Leading Social Trading network. Copy profitable traders – or become a 'leader' and earn when other traders follow your trades.

Software Strategies

Choosing the right software is a hugely important decision, but part of that decision comes with ensuring that it works harmoniously with your day trading strategies. If you're trading forex using a simple price action strategy, then you may have everything you need with your broker's standard program software. Tools such as TradingView can also help you build and backtest strategies, including using your code if desired.

However, if you have a complex strategy you may need software that has all the indicators and technical tools at a few clicks notice, to ensure you make fast and accurate decisions. Your strategy needs are likely to be greater and you may require optional advanced features that are often expensive.

Demo Accounts

If you want to test a specific software before committing to it, the best way to do it is a "demo account". A demo account is a form of practice account where you trade for free with "play money" using the real software and its features. It's a great way to trial software, strategies, and skills and is something we highly recommend. We list all trading demo accounts here.

- ❖ Regional Impact
- ❖ Tailored for specific markets

The best trading software for Australia and Canada may fall short of the mark in Indian and South African markets. This is simply because the software in India can be extremely different to Australian software. Spider software, for example, provides technical analysis software specifically for Indian markets. But if you want to trade stocks in the West, you may find that software from far afield won't give you all the access to data feeds and news resources you need to successfully trade.

There's also the question of cost. You can get plenty of free charting software for Indian markets, but the same powerful and comprehensive software in the UK, Europe, and the US can often come with a hefty price tag. So, make sure your software comparison takes into account location and price.

Tax Considerations

The same principle applies to day trading tax software. The accounting software needs to be able to accurately calculate how much tax is payable to your country's specific body, the IRS for example. Apart from wasting your time, any tax errors will fall on your lap, as will any fines.

Final Word On Location

If you're British, do your homework and find out what the best trading software specifically for the UK is. If you're Canadian, check you won't encounter any tax problems if you invest in accounting software from South Africa.

Take-Home Points

It's worth bearing in mind that your choice of broker can restrict the tools available to you. Free day trading software may seem like a no brainer to start with, but if it comes with the sacrifice of technical tools that could enhance trade decisions then it may cost you in the long run. Remember the best day trading software for forex may not cut the mustard when you use it for stocks, so do your research and consider all the factors outlined above. Most importantly, you wouldn't buy a car without test driving it first, and your day trading software shouldn't be any different.

Best Day Trading Software:

- TD Ameritrade: Best for resources
- Interactive Brokers: Best for high-volume traders
- E-Trade: Best for intermediate to advanced traders
- Charles Schwab: Best for premium features
- eOption: Best for advanced traders
- Tradespoon: Best for all levels
- Yewno|Edge: Best for alternative data
- TradeStation: Best for usability

Risks And Potential Of Day Trading

Professional day traders are drawn to the benefits of day trading, which can include:

Work From Home Opportunities: Day traders are often attracted to the freedom of location especially for parents of young children, those who care for family members or students.

Virtually Unlimited Earning Potential: Forget waiting for a raise or fighting coworkers for a promotion. So long as you choose liquid assets that can be easily bought and sold, the only limit to your income is the success of your trading strategy.

Independence: Day traders never have to worry about someone stealing their idea at a meeting or dealing with a difficult boss. Many day traders report a huge amount of personal satisfaction from being personally responsible for all of their income and losses.

Some Of The Risks Of Day Trading Include:

Capital Losses: Even if a majority of trades are profitable, day traders may see commissions, fees, and minor losses slowly chip away at their profits, which results in less money earned.

A Lack Of Guaranteed Income: If you have a family to support, a guaranteed income is likely very high on your list of needs to provide for your family. The unpredictability of the market and the potential for trading loss can cause undue amounts of stress.

High Barrier To Market Entry: Pattern day traders must have at least $25,000 in their accounts before they may begin trading on the margin (even if their brokerage's minimum is lower than this amount) according to regulations from the SEC.

Psychological Addiction: It can be easy to get addicted to the action. The connection between trading and gambling addiction is so strong that Gamblers Anonymous has a recommendation that traders hold a stock for at least 18 months before selling if they hold stock at all.

What Makes A Good Day Trading Software?

Before you choose what day trading platform, you should know what separates great brokerages from okay ones.

Low Fees And Commissions

Unlike investing for retirement (which typically involves purchasing a stock or fund and holding onto it for years), day traders make a large number of trades per month, sometimes executing upwards of ten trades a day. This means that fees and commission prices should be more important today traders than long-term buyers. Even a few dollars' difference in commission price can make a huge impact for active traders.

A Comprehensive And Responsive Platform

Day traders (especially those that scalp and sell as soon as their assets become profitable) rely on quick movements to make money on their trades. The best day trading platforms are responsive and employ an up-to-date research center to help traders plan more effectively and quickly buy and sell their shares. Trading platforms should be easy to use and intuitive—check out a few YouTube tutorials before committing to ensure that you understand where the most important tools on your platform are located and how to operate them.

Minimum Account Balances

Most platforms have some type of minimum balance, ranging from $500 for basic accounts to $10,000 for professional trading platforms. Make sure you have enough capital to meet the account minimum before you sign up for a platform.

Great Research Tools

Research tools, like market analyses, expert editorials, and market movement news can also be particularly beneficial for day traders. The best trading platforms also offer daily news and research over a breath of multiple asset types and industries to offer you a full picture of how the market will move daily.

Mobile Compatibility

Do you frequently trade on the go? Some brokerages offer mobile trading platforms for smartphones and tablets that will allow you to trade away from your desktop an invaluable benefit for full-time traders who want to watch their charts 24/7.

The Best Day Trading Software

1. TD Ameritrade

TD Ameritrade offers a large number of tools and platform options to make day trading simple and profitable. The brokerage's online desktop platform offers a host of learning tools for new traders, including a full library of educational videos and articles, portfolio planning tools, and even a chatbot that can answer questions on demand.

TD Ameritrade's expert-level thinkorswim platform offers advanced charting software, customizable trading indicators, and practice trading with a dummy account called paperMoney. Mobile traders will fall in love with the TD Ameritrade Mobile Trader app, which offers almost the same functionality as its desktop counterpart.

Unfortunately for day traders, this extensive research database and tools come at a price TD Ameritrade customers will pay $6.95 per trade, which is quite high and can seriously cut into profits.

However, the platform has a $0 account minimum and charges no annual or inactivity fees.

2. Interactive Brokers

Interactive Brokers' platform was created with the active, professional day trader in mind. The platform is not intended for casual or long-term traders. If you want to open an account with Interactive Brokers, you'll need to pay a $10 monthly inactivity fee if you do not keep at least $100,000 in your account or you do not accumulate at least $10 in monthly trade commissions.

While $10 may not sound like a lot, consider the fact that other brokers charge between $4 and $7 per trade and Interactive Brokers' commissions are the lowest in the game. You can expect to pay $0.005 per share traded with a minimum of $1 and a maximum of 1% of the trade value.

Interactive Brokers even offer additional discounts for the highest-volume traders. The broker's Trader Workstation is an extensive and overwhelmingly large number of intricate features, including volatility measurement tools, customizable alerts and watchlists, and "heat maps" of market segments that experience unusual activity. With a massive selection of stocks, rock-bottom fees, and high-level trading tools, Interactive Brokers is a powerful tool in the hands of an experienced day trader but may be overly complicated and expensive for new traders.

3. E-Trade

You might remember E-Trade from the brokerage's "trading baby" commercials that were popular in the early 2000s but the platform has expanded its offerings exponentially since that time. E-Trade now offers three platforms aimed at a specific segment of traders: E-trade Web, OptionsHouse, and E-Trade Pro. E-Trade Pro offers the highest number of features and analysis tools, but access is restricted to those who hold an account with at least $250,000 in the capital. The E-Trade mobile app is simple, yet responsive, and allows traders to place orders and track real-time stock quotes with little lag or delay. E-Trade's commissions are a bit more expensive than most at $6.95 a trade, but new traders can often get 60 days of free trading when they open an account with at least a $10,000 minimum deposit.

4. Charles Schwab

Charles Schwab offers a brokerage suite perfect for traders of all skill levels, capital, and research needs. New day traders will appreciate Charles Schwab's easy-to-use Trade Source trading platform and 24/7 customer service options while seasoned veterans will love the broker's customizable StreetSmart Edge platform and extensive research options, live news and earning reports and in-house equity ratings. The broker's mobile app also offers above-average functionality, with a fast and responsive interface and simple trading options. However, it's important to note that opening an account with Charles Schwab requires an initial minimum deposit of $1,000 though this fee is often waived with promotions and monthly $100 deposits.

5. eOption

eOption is the broker for day traders who are concerned about costs above all else. At just $3 commission per trade and a $500 minimum balance, eruptions costs are hard to beat without moving up to a professional-grade broker like Interactive Brokers. eOption offers both a desktop and mobile platform, each with full trading functionality, live streams, and up-to-date quotes.

However, the platform compensates for this low commission in other ways "inactive traders" who make fewer than two trades per year or who have less than $10,000 in the capital in their accounts will face a $50 annual fee, and the broker cuts many of the research and analysis tools that characterize more expensive options. eOption is best for advanced brokers who use outside charting and research tools and only need the trading platform to execute their buys and sells.

6. Tradespoon

Tradespoon is designed for both beginners, advanced and intermediate traders looking to further their growth on the platform. Tradespoon is dynamic in the sense that it offers traders the educational resources necessary to enhance trading intelligence. Its user-friendly software entails screenings of the market in its entirety, which is favorable in terms of both optimal and stock trading. Tradespoon also offers one-on-one mentoring, so you're never left in the dark. With one-on-one assistance, you'll be able to ease into the profitable opportunities of the market.

7. Yewno|Edge

Yewno|Edge is a research platform that leverages Yewno's proprietary AI and Knowledge Graph Technology to enhance traditional technical and fundamental stock research with alternative data. Its modular and component-based approach allows you to build and customize a workspace that has all the important data-points you'll need to monitor your portfolio in real-time. Switch between idea generation workspace with Stock Screener and Strategy Builder to learn about the concepts you care about and identify new opportunities.

8. TradeStation

TradeStation's platform used to only be best for professional traders who needed a highly technical platform. Now, with TradeStation's new TS GO account option, novice traders will have access to professional-grade stock screeners and extensive educational and development tools to help them develop as investors. Another strength of TradeStation is the number of offerings available to trade. From stocks to ETFs to futures contracts to cryptocurrencies, TradeStation offers a wide variety of tradable assets. These assets are complemented by a host of educational tools and resources. Furthermore, as is the case with other brokerages on this list. TradeStation offers $0 commissions on stocks and most ETFs.

Chapter 8 - Markets Risk

What Is Market Risk?

Looking for a market risk definition? The place to start is the name itself. Market risk is a type of risk associated with the market as a whole rather than with individual stocks or business sectors. In other words, it is the risk that the market overall will lose value, rather than that one or more stocks or sectors will go out of favor to be replaced by those upon whom investors are smiling. Market risk is the possibility of an investor experiencing losses due to factors that affect the overall performance of the financial markets in which he or she is involved. Market risk, also called "systematic risk," cannot be eliminated through diversification, though it can be hedged against in other ways. Sources of market risk include recessions, political turmoil, changes in interest rates, natural disasters, and terrorist attacks. Systematic, or market risk tends to influence the entire market at the same time.

Where Have You Heard About Market Risk?

As an investor, you will be alert to market risk even if you don't yet use the market risk definition. Panics and crashes on Wall Street and elsewhere are part of market lore. Everyone has heard of tulip-mania, the Wall Street Crash, and Black Monday. Your financial adviser will be on the lookout for signs of a bubble likely to burst, and financial media will scan the horizon for common causes of market risk including interest-rate risk, equity-price risk, commodity risk, and foreign exchange risk.

What You Need To Know About Market Risk...

Market risk is also known as systematic risk and undiversifiable risk. The word 'systematic' refers to the way such risk affects the whole market, systematically threatening share prices. Such a risk is unverifiable because, by definition, it is impossible to seek safety in a diversified portfolio when every element of that portfolio is facing the same risk.

The Definition Of 'Market Risk'

Market risk is the risk that the value of an investment will decrease due to changes in market factors. These factors will have an impact on the overall performance of the financial markets and can only be reduced by diversification into assets that are not correlated with the market – such as certain alternative asset classes.

Market risk is sometimes called "systematic risk" because it relates to factors, such as a recession, that impact the entire market. Several different risk factors make up market risk.

Currency Risk: The risk that exchange rates will go up or possibly down

Equity Risk: The risk that share prices will go up or down

Inflation Risk: the potential for inflation to increase the price of all goods and services such that it undermines the value of money

Commodity Risk: The possibility of commodity prices such as metals change value dramatically

Interest Rate Risk: The risk that comes from an increase or decrease in interest rates

Understanding Market Risk

Market (systematic) risk and specific risk (unsystematic) make up the two major categories of investment risk. The most common types of market risks include interest rate risk, equity risk, currency risk, and commodity risk.

Publicly traded companies in the United States are required by the Securities and Exchange Commission (SEC) to disclose how their productivity and results may be linked to the performance of the financial markets. This requirement is meant to detail a company's exposure to financial risk. For example, a company providing derivative investments or foreign exchange futures may be more exposed to financial risk than companies that do not provide these types of investments. This information helps investors and traders make decisions based on their own risk management rules.

In contrast to market risk, specific risk or "unsystematic risk" is tied directly to the performance of a particular security and can be protected against through investment diversification. One example of unsystematic risk is a company declaring bankruptcy, thereby making it's stock worthless to investors.

What Are The Primary Sources Of Market Risk?

Market risk is the risk of loss due to the factors that affect an entire market or asset class. Market risk is also known as undiversifiable risk because it affects all asset classes and is unpredictable. An investor can only mitigate this type of risk by hedging a portfolio. Four primary sources of risk affect the overall market: interest rate risk, equity price risk, foreign exchange risk, and commodity risk.

Interest Rate Risk

Interest rate risk is the risk of increased volatility due to a change in interest rates. There are different types of risk exposures that can arise when there is a change of interest rates, such as basis risk, options risk, term structure risk, and repricing risk. Basis risk is a component due to possible changes in spreads when interest rates are fluctuating. Basis risk arises when there are changes in the spread between different markets' interest rates.

Equity Price Risk

Equity price risk is the risk that arises from security price volatility – the risk of a decline in the value of a security or a portfolio. Equity price risk can be either systematic or unsystematic risk. Unsystematic risk can be mitigated through diversification, whereas systematic cannot be. In a global economic crisis, equity price risk is systematic because it affects multiple asset classes. A portfolio can only be hedged against this risk. For example, if an investor is invested in multiple assets that represent an index, the investor can hedge against equity price risk by buying put options in the index exchange-traded fund.

Foreign Exchange Risk

Currency risk, or foreign exchange risk, is a form of risk that arises when currency exchange rates are volatile. Global firms may be exposed to currency risk when conducting business due to imperfect hedges.

For example, suppose a U.S investor has investments in China. The realized return will be affected when exchanging the two currencies. Assume the investor has a realized 50% return on investment in China, but the Chinese yuan depreciates 20% against the U.S. dollar. Due to the change in currencies, the investor will only have a 30% return. This risk can be mitigated by hedging with currency exchange-traded funds.

Commodity Risk

Commodity price risk is the volatility in market price due to the price fluctuation of a commodity. Commodity risk affects various sectors of the market, such as airlines and casino gaming. A commodity's price is affected by politics, seasonal changes, technology, and current market conditions.

For example, suppose there is an oversupply of crude oil, which has caused oil prices to fall every day over the past six months. A company that is heavily invested in oil drilling wells faces commodity price risk. The company's profit margin will fall as well since it is still operating at the same cost, but the prices of crude oil are falling. Its profits will decrease. The company could use it

Risk Management And Stock Market

In the stock market, there is a strong relationship between risk and return. Greater the risk, greater the return generally! In financial terminology risk management is the process of identifying and assessing the risk and then developing strategies to manage and minimize the same while maximizing the returns.

Every investment demands a certain amount of risk and for an investor to assume this risk he has to be compensated duly. This compensation is in the form of something called the risk premium or simply the premium. Risk is therefore central to stock markets or investing because without risk there can be no gains. Successful investors use stock market risk management strategies to minimize the risk and maximize the gain.

In financial markets there are generally two types of risk; first the Market risk and second the Inflation risk. Market risk results from the possibility of an increase or decrease in financial markets. The other risk i.e. the Inflation or the purchasing power risk results from the rise and fall of prices of goods and services over time.

The inflation risk is an important consideration in long term investments whereas the market risk is more relevant in the short term. It is the market risk that can be managed and controlled to a certain extent, inflation risk cannot be controlled. Certain strategies can be employed to mitigate the risk in a stock market.

The Strategies Are As Follows:

1. Follow The Trend Of The Market: This is one of the proven methods to minimize risks in a stock market. The problem is that it is difficult to spot trends in the market and trends change very fast. A market trend may last a single day, a month or a year, and again short term trends operate within long term trends.

2. Portfolio Diversification: Another useful risk management strategy in the stock market is to diversify your risk by investing in a portfolio. In a portfolio, you diversify your investment to several companies, sectors, and asset classes. There is a probability that while the market value of a certain investment decreases that of the other may increase. Mutual Funds are yet another means to diversify the impact.

3. Stop Loss: Stop loss or trailing tool is yet another device to check that you don't lose money should the stock go far a fall. In this strategy, the investor has the option of exiting if a certain stock falls below a certain specified limit. Self-discipline is yet another option employed by some investors to sell when the stock falls below a certain level or when there is a steep fall.

7 Common Types Of Risk Involved In Stocks

Here are 7 common types of risk involved in stocks that every stock investor should know:

1. Market Risk

This is also called systematic risk and is based on the day-to-day price fluctuation in the market. The market index Sensex and Nifty goes up and down throughout the day. And many a time, it may affect the returns from a stock. For example, if the market is going down at a time, then it might pull down the prices of even some good stocks. Moreover, in the short term, market risks are higher compared to the long term.

2. Business Risk

The second type of stock risk comes from the business. This risk can be escalated if the business is not doing well. Reasons like the failure of management, poor quarter-by-quarter results, or your misjudgment in picking a company come under business risk. However, you can mitigate this risk by diversification. The chance of one business not performing well is 'high' compared to 5 such companies. Hence, if you are keeping 5 stocks in your portfolio, instead of one, you can reduce the business risk.

3. Liquidity Risk

Before investing in a stock, you should check how solvent the company is? Companies with high debts may find it hard to pay their bills. Many times, they might even cut the dividends or in the worst case, may go bankrupt. Liquidity risks are involved in all businesses.

4. Taxability Risk

The government changes taxes all the time and hence taxes may increase or decrease in the particular industry where you invested. The change in taxation can affect the stock price.

Further, few industries are taxed comparatively higher to others and hence, their net profit after tax may be less. Further, as taxation is controlled by the government, there is not much that the management or the investors can do.

For example, I'm holding the stock of ITC. During July of last year (2017), the stock price of the company fell over 15% in a day due to news of an increase in taxation after GST in the cigarettes. A big chunk of my profit was gone that day and I couldn't do much about it. I didn't sell ITC because I bought it at an even cheaper price and am still bullish on this stock for the long-run.

However, before investing in this cigarette-giant company, I always knew this might happen and was willing to take the risk. Further, as a back plan, I had diversified my portfolio, which means that although ITC was down, however, other stocks in my portfolio were doing great. Therefore, the overall impact on my portfolio due to the poor performance of just one stock was quite small.

5. Interest Rate Risk

The open market or global market interest rates changes from time to time. And this can positively or adversely affect the stocks depending on the direction in which the interest rate is moving. For example, when the interest rates are high, a company might find it difficult to borrow money (at high rates). Further, the bond market declines as the interest rate increases, which may also affect the corporate bonds.

6. Regulatory Risks

There are several regulations imposed in the different industry which must also be termed as the risk involved in stocks. For example, Cigarettes, telecommunication, beverages, pharmaceutical, and a few other industries are highly regulated. If a pharmaceutical company loses any of its drug manufacturing right/permission because of a regulatory effect, then it will affect the company's profit and hence, the stock price.

7. Inflationary Risk

With an increase in inflation, the price of raw material will increase, which can affect the production cost. Many companies involved in commodities like oil, soya bean, etc are affected a lot by inflationary risk.

Further, for a few industries, the inflation rate is too high. For example, education and healthcare.

The tuition fee for schools and colleges are increasing at a very fast rate. Although, it might sound good in the short term as these industries will make money from the inflated price. However, in the long run, it might harm the retention of the customers.

Bonus: A Few Other Risks

Besides the above mentioned 7 risks involved in stocks, here are few other risks that are worth mentioning.

1. Social And Political Risk: Many companies face problems due to social and political risks. For example, Tata Motors shifted its Tata-Nano plant from West-Bengal to Sanand- Gujarat because of political reasons, which cost a lot of money to Tata.

2. Credit Risk: The risk that the company who issued the bond won't be able to pay the interest or repay the principal at maturity and may find it hard to buy/sell goods.

3. FII/DII Investments: The investment by big players can also be counted as the risk involved in stocks. If the foreign direct investment/ domestic investment decreases in a company, and they start selling their stocks, then it might adversely affect the share price of that company.

4. Currency And Exchange Rate Risk: Many companies who deals across nations or the companies involved in import/export may face a problem with increased dollar price. Therefore, the currency and exchange rate fluctuations might increase risk in these companies.

Closing Thoughts

There are several risks involved in stocks. Nevertheless, if you understand the basic concept behind the risk involved in stocks, you can control the amount of risk you want to take. Moreover, the risk is reduced over the long-term. A short-term fluctuation won't hurt your portfolio in the long run. Further, most of the short-term market fluctuations, political, or social risks will be nullified while investing for 10-15 years.

Overall, yes!! There are several risks involved in the stock market. Nevertheless, risk-takers are awarded in the stock market if you take 'smart' calculated risk.

Chapter 9 - Risk And Reward Ratio

What Is the Risk/Reward Ratio?

The risk/reward ratio marks the prospective reward an investor can earn, for every dollar, he or she risks an investment. Many investors use risk/reward ratios to compare the expected returns of an investment with the amount of risk they must undertake to earn these returns. Consider the following example: an investment with a risk-reward ratio of 1:7 suggests that an investor is willing to risk $1, for the prospect of earning $7. Alternatively, a risk/reward ratio of 1:3 signals that an investor should expect to invest $1, for the prospect of earning $3 on his investment. Traders often use this approach to plan which trades to take, and the ratio is calculated by dividing the amount a trader stands to lose if the price of an asset moves in an unexpected direction (the risk) by the amount of profit the trader expects to have made when the position is closed (the reward).

Facts

The risk/reward ratio is used by traders to manage their capital and risk of loss during trading. The ratio helps assess the expected return and risk of a given trade. A good risk-reward ratio tends to be anything greater than 1 in 3.

How The Risk/Reward Ratio Works

The risk/reward ratio is often used as a measure when trading individual stocks. The optimal risk/reward ratio differs widely among various trading strategies. Some trial-and-error methods are usually required to determine which ratio is best for a given trading strategy, and many investors have a pre-specified risk/reward ratio for their investments.

In many cases, market strategists find the ideal risk/reward ratio for their investments to be approximately 1:3, or three units of expected return for every one unit of additional risk. Investors can manage risk/reward more directly through the use of stop-loss orders and derivatives such as put options.

What Does the Risk/Reward Ratio Tell You?

The risk/reward ratio helps investors manage their risk of losing money on trades. Even if a trader has some profitable trades, he will lose money over time if his win rate is below 50%. The risk/reward ratio measures the difference between a trade entry point to stop-loss and a sell or take-profit order. Comparing these two provides the ratio of profit to loss, or reward to risk.

Investors often use stop-loss orders when trading individual stocks to help minimize losses and directly manage their investments with a risk/reward focus. A stop-loss order is a trading trigger placed on a stock that automates the selling of the stock from a portfolio if the stock reaches a specified low. Investors can automatically set stop-loss orders through brokerage accounts and typically do not require exorbitant additional trading costs.

Example Of The Risk/Reward Ratio In Use

Consider this example: A trader purchases 100 shares of XYZ Company at $20 and places a stop-loss order at $15 to ensure that losses will not exceed $500. Also, assume that this trader believes that the price of XYZ will reach $30 in the next few months. In this case, the trader is willing to risk $5 per share to make an expected return of $10 per share after closing the position. Since the trader stands to make double the amount that she has risked, she would be said to have a 1:2 risk/reward ratio on that particular trade. Derivatives contracts such as put contracts, which give their owners the right to sell the underlying asset at a specified price, can be used to similar effect.

If a more conservative investor seeks a 1:5 risk/reward ratio for a specified investment (five units of expected return for each additional unit of risk), then he can use the stop-loss order to adjust the risk/reward ratio to his specification. In this case, in the trading example noted above, if an investor has a 1:5 risk/reward ratio required for his investment, he would set the stop-loss order at $18 instead of $15 that is, he is more risk-averse.

What Is Calculating Risk And Reward?

Are you a risk-taker? When you're an individual trader in the stock market, one of the few safety devices you have is the risk/reward calculation. The actual calculation to determine risk vs. reward is very easy. You simply divide your net profit (the reward) by the price of your maximum risk. Calculate risk vs. reward by dividing your net profit (the reward) by the price of your maximum risk.

Understanding Risk vs. Reward

Sadly, retail investors might end up losing a lot of money when they try to invest their own money. There are many reasons for this, but one of those comes from the inability of individual investors to manage risk. Risk/reward is a common term in financial vernacular, but what does it mean?

Calculating Risk And Reward

To incorporate risk/reward calculations into your research, pick a stock; set the upside and downside targets based on the current price; calculate the risk/reward; if it is below your threshold, raise your downside target to attempt to achieve an acceptable ratio; if you can't achieve an acceptable ratio, start with a different investment.

Investing money into the markets has a high degree of risk and you should be compensated if you're going to take that risk. If somebody you marginally trust asks for a $50 loan and offers to pay you $60 in two weeks, it might not be worth the risk, but what if they offered to pay you $100? The risk of losing $50 for the chance to make $100 might be appealing.

That's a 2:1 risk/reward, which is a ratio where a lot of professional investors start to get interested because it allows investors to double their money. Similarly, if the person offered you $150, then the ratio goes to 3:1.

Now let's look at this in terms of the stock market. Assume you did your research and found a stock you like. You notice that XYZ stock is trading at $25, down from a recent high of $29.

You believe that if you buy now, in the not-so-distant future, XYZ will go back up to $29, and you can cash in. You have $500 to put toward this investment, so you buy 20 shares. You did all of your research, but do you know your risk/reward ratio? If you're like most individual investors, you probably don't.

Before we learn if our XYZ trade is a good idea from a risk perspective, what else should we know about this risk/reward ratio? First, although a little bit of behavioral economics finds its way into most investment decisions, risk/reward is completely objective. It's a calculation and the numbers don't lie.

Second, each individual has their tolerance for risk. You may love bungee jumping, but somebody else might have a panic attack just thinking about it.

Next, risk/reward gives you no indication of probability. What if you took your $500 and played the lottery? Risking $500 to gain millions is a much better investment than investing in the stock market from a risk/reward perspective, but a much worse choice in terms of probability.

In the course of holding a stock, the upside number is likely to change as you continue analyzing new information. If the risk/reward becomes unfavorable, don't be afraid to exit the trade. Never find yourself in a situation where the risk/reward ratio isn't in your favor.

The Calculation

Remember, to calculate risk/reward, you divide your net profit (the reward) by the price of your maximum risk. Using the XYZ example above, if your stock went up to $29 per share, you would make $4 for each of your 20 shares for a total of $80. You paid $500 for it, so you would divide 80 by 500 which gives you 0.16.

That means that your risk/reward for this idea is 0.16:1. Most professional investors won't give the idea a second look at such a low risk/reward ratio, so this is a terrible idea. Or is it?

The Steps

To incorporate risk/reward calculations into your research, follow these steps:

- Pick a stock using exhaustive research.
- Set the upside and downside targets based on the current price.
- Calculate the risk/reward.
- If it is below your threshold, raise your downside target to attempt to achieve an acceptable ratio.
- If you can't achieve an acceptable ratio, start over with a different investment idea.

Once you start incorporating risk/reward, you will quickly notice that it's difficult to find good investment or trade ideas. The pros comb through, sometimes, hundreds of charts each day looking for ideas that fit their risk/reward profile. Don't shy away from this. The more meticulous you are, the better your chances of making money.

Let's Get Real (Limiting Risk And Stop Losses)

Unless you're an inexperienced stock investor, you would never let that $500 go all the way to zero. Your actual risk isn't the entire $500.

Every good investor has a stop-loss or a price on the downside that limits their risk. If you set a $29 sell limit price as the upside, maybe you set $20 as the maximum downside. Once your stop-loss order reaches $20, you sell it and look for the next opportunity.

Because we limited our downside, we can now change our numbers a bit. Your new profit stays the same at $80, but your risk is now only $100 ($5 maximum loss multiplied by the 20 shares that you own), or 80/100 = 0.8:1. This is still not ideal.

What if we raised our stop-loss price to $23, risking only $2 per share or $40 loss in total? Remember, 80/40 is 2:1, which is acceptable. Some investors won't commit their money to any investment that isn't at least 4:1, but 2:1 is considered the minimum by most. Of course, you have to decide for yourself what the acceptable ratio is for you.

Notice that to achieve the risk/reward profile of 2:1, we didn't change the top number. When you did your research and concluded that the maximum upside was $29, that was based on technical analysis and fundamental research. If we were to change the top number, to achieve an acceptable risk/reward, we're now relying on hope instead of good research.

Every good investor knows that relying on hope is a losing proposition. Being more conservative with your risk is always better than being more aggressive with your reward. Risk/reward is always calculated realistically, yet conservatively.

Using The Risk/Reward Ratio In Trading

The risk/reward ratio is used to assess the profit potential of a trade relative to its loss potential. To attain the risk and reward of trade, both the risk and profit potential of a trade must be defined by the trader. Risk is determined using a stop-loss order, where the risk is the price difference between the entry point of the trade and the stop-loss order. A profit target is used to establish an exit point should the trade move favorably. The potential profit for the trade is the price difference between the profit target and the entry price.

If a trader buys a stock at $25.60, places a stop loss at $25.50 and a profit target at $25.85, then the risk on the trade is $0.10 ($25.60 - $25.50) and the profit potential is $0.25 ($25.85 - $25.60).

The risk is then compared to the profit to create the ratio: risk/reward = $0.10 / $0.25 = 0.4

If the ratio is great than 1.0, the risk is greater than the profit potential on the trade. If the ratio is less than 1.0, the profit potential is greater than the risk.

Closer Look At The Risk/Reward Ratio

By itself, it appears that low risk/ratios of 0.1 or 0.2 are better, however, that is not necessarily the case. Traders must also consider the odds that their profit target will be reached before their stop loss. You can make any trade look attractive by putting your profit target far away from the entry point, but how often will the market reach that lofty target before reaching the much closer stop loss level?

Therefore, there is a balancing act between taking trades that offer more profit than risk, but where the trade still has a reasonable chance of reaching the target before the stop loss. For most day traders, risk/reward ratios typically fall between 1.0 and 0.25, although there are exceptions. Day traders, swing traders, and investors should shy away from trades where the profit potential is less than what they are putting at risk, for example, a risk/reward greater than 1.0. There are enough favorable opportunities available that there is little reason to take on more risk for less profit.

When establishing the risk/reward for a trade, place the stop loss at a logical place on the chart according to your strategy, then place a logical profit target based on your strategy/analysis. These levels should not be randomly chosen. When the stop loss and profit target locations are established, only then assess the risk/reward of the trade and decide if the trade is worth taking. A common mistake is that traders have a certain risk/reward ratio in mind. For example, they may only want to risk $0.05 to make $0.20 and so they enter the trade anywhere and place a stop loss $0.05 away and a profit target $0.20 away. While this may occasionally work, it is not an ideal way to trade.

To trade effectively, have a trading plan in place that tells you exactly when and where to enter a trade and where to place your stop loss levels and targets under various market conditions. Then have a rule that stipulates that you only take trades that produce a risk/reward ratio of a certain number or lower.

Final Word On The Risk/Reward Ratio

In isolation, it is typically better to take trades that have lower risk/reward ratios, as that means the profit potential outweighs the risk. The risk/reward doesn't need to be very low to be effective, though; anything below 1.0 is likely to produce better results than taking trades with a greater than 1.0 risk/reward ratio. The risk/reward ratio is often used in combination with other risk management ratios, such as the win/loss ratio, which compares the number of winning and losing trades, and the break-even percentage, which gives the number of winning trades that are required to break even.

Chapter 10 - Investment Income ?

What Is Investment Income?

Investment income is income that comes from interest payments, dividends, capital gains collected upon the sale of a security or other assets, and any other profit made through an investment vehicle of any kind. Generally, individuals earn most of their total net income each year through regular employment income. However, disciplined saving and investment in the financial markets can grow moderate savings into large investment portfolios, yielding an investor a large annual investment income over time. Interest earned on bank accounts, dividends received from stock owned by mutual fund holdings, or sales of gold coins held in a safety deposit box would all be considered investment income. Often, income made on investments undergoes different, and sometimes preferential, tax treatment, which varies by country and locality.

Businesses also often have income from investments. On the income statements of publicly traded companies, an item called the investment "income or losses" is commonly listed. This is where the company reports the portion of the net income obtained through investments made with surplus cash, as opposed to being earned with the company's usual line of business. For a business, this may include all of the above, as well as interest earned or lost on its bonds that have been issued, share buybacks, corporate spinoffs, and acquisitions.

Facts

Investment income is income that is earned from investments, such as real estate and the stock market. Investment income is taxed at a different rate once it is withdrawn as compared to regular income.

Understanding Investment Income

Investment income refers solely to the financial gains above the original cost of the investment. The form the income takes, such as interest or dividend payments, is irrelevant to it being considered investment income as long as the income is generated from a previous investment. Additionally, investment income can be received as a lump sum or regular interest payments paid out over time.

Investment Income Made Simple

In the simplest form, the interest accrued on a basic savings account is considered income. The interest is generated as an amount above and beyond the original investments, which are the deposits placed into the account, making it a source of income. Options, stocks, and bonds can also generate investment income.

Whether this is through regular interest or dividend payments or selling a security at a higher rate than it was purchased, the funds above the original cost of the investment qualify as investment income.

Understanding Investment Properties

Real estate transactions can also be considered investment income, and some investors choose to purchase real estate specifically as a way to generate investment income - either from the cash flows generated from rents or any capital gains experienced when selling the property. Once the original cost of the property is repaid by the investor, and rent payments received are not used for the purpose of covering other property-related expenses, the income qualifies as investment income.

Investment Income And Taxes

While it is not always the case, the majority of investment income is subject to a preferred level of taxation once the funds are withdrawn. The associated tax rate is based on the form of investment producing the income and other aspects of an individual taxpayer's situation. Many retirement accounts, such as a 401(k) or traditional IRA, are subject to taxation once the funds are withdrawn. Certain tax-favorable investments, such as a Roth IRA, are not taxed on eligible gains associated with a qualified distribution.

For example, currently, in the U.S., the top marginal tax rate on income is 37 percent (for amounts over $500,000 a year). Meanwhile, long-term capital gains and qualified dividend income is subject only to a maximum 20 percent tax, even if that amount exceeds a half-million dollars in a given year.

Investment income can also be used in conjunction with an individual's earnings to provide income tax credits. For example, one of the criteria used to evaluate individuals for the Earned Income Tax Credit (EITC) is to earn from running a small business and do not have an investment income of over $3,500.

Examples Of Investment Income

Suppose an individual buys stocks of company ABC for $50. Two weeks later, she sells them for $70, netting a profit of $20 in the process. Then the income she earned from her investment in company ABC is considered investment income and taxed accordingly. Suppose the same individual invests $500,000 in real estate property. She sells the property for $1.5 million ten years later. Then her investment is categorized as investment income and taxed based on long term capital gains tax.

Steps To Successful Income Investing For Beginners

Do you need to build a portfolio that will generate cash? Are you more concerned with paying your bills and having enough income than growing richer? If so, you should consider using an older investing technique—income investing.

This long-lost practice used to be popular before the great twenty-year bull market taught everyone to believe that the only good investment was one that you bought for $10 and sold for $20. Although income investing went out of style with the general public, the discipline is still quietly practiced throughout the mahogany-paneled offices of the most respected wealth management firms in the world.

Income investing is the practice of designing a portfolio of diversified investments to achieve a passive income to live on. These investments can include real estate, stocks, mutual funds, and bonds. It is important to consider which types of assets might be most valuable to someone who wanted to follow an income investing philosophy and understand the most common dangers that can affect an income investing portfolio

Chapter 11 - Basic Stock Markets Terms For Beginners

Stock Trading Terms Every Trader Needs to Know

What Do Stock Trading Terms Mean?

Stock market terms are industry-specific jargon for the securities industry. When experts and amateurs talk about trading stocks, they use these stock market terms to speak specifically about strategies, charts, patterns, indices, and other elements of the stock trading industry. Learning stock market terms will allow you to accelerate the learning process. I tell my Trading Challenge students over and over again to do their research first. If you're knowledgeable about the stock market, you stand to profit far more than if you trade based on instinct or "hot picks."

Some stock market terms such as bull and bear, which I'll cover below also apply to other investment vehicles, such as real estate. I'm only going to cover their relationship to stocks, but you might see them pop up in other conversations.

Key Basic Stock Market Terms

Let's look at some of the most important stock market terms you'll encounter as you learn how to trade stocks. Feel free to bookmark this page so you can return to it later as a handy reference. Are you learning about investing? Then you must learn and understand some basic investment terminology. Here is a list of some basic investing terms you should know, along with their definition:

1. Annual Report

An annual report is a report prepared by a company that's intended to impress shareholders. It contains tons of information about the company, from its cash flow to its management strategy. When you read an annual report, you're judging the company's solvency and financial situation.

2. Arbitrage

Arbitrage refers to buying and selling the same security in different markets and at different price points. For instance, if stock XYZ is trading at $10 on one market and $10.50 on another, the trader could buy X shares for $10 and sell them for $10.50 on the other market, pocketing the difference.

3. Averaging Down

When an investor buys more of a stock as the price goes down. This makes it so your average purchase price decreases. You might use this strategy if you believe that the consensus about a company is wrong, so you expect the stock price to rebound later.

4. Bear Market

Gold cast statuette depicting a stylized bull and a bear in dramatic contrasting light representing financial market trends created by

Inked Pixels – Shutterstock.com Trading talk for the stock market being in a downward trend, or a period of falling stock prices. This is the opposite of a bull market. If a stock price plummets, it's very bearish.

. Beta

A measurement of the relationship between the price of a stock and the movement of the whole market. If stock XYZ has a beta of 1.5, that means that for every 1 point move in the market, stock XYZ moves 1.5 points and vice versa.

6. Blue Chip Stocks

The stocks behind large, industry-leading companies. Blue-chip stocks offer a stable record of significant dividend payments and have a reputation for sound fiscal management. The expression is thought to have been derived from blue gambling chips, which is the highest denomination of chips used in casinos.

7. Bourse

This stock market term is a little murky. Technically, it's just another name for the stock market and originates from a house in which wealthy men gathered to trade shares. However, when you hear it in today's conversations about the stock market, it usually either refers to the Paris stock exchange or a non-U.S. stock exchange.

8. Bull Market

When the stock market as a whole is in a prolonged period of increasing stock prices. It's the opposite of a bear market. A single stock can be bullish or bearish too, as can a sector, which I'll describe later on.

9. Broker

A person who buys or sells an investment for you in exchange for a fee (a commission).

10. Bid

The bid is the amount of money a trader is willing to pay per share for a given stock. It's balanced against the asking price, which is what a seller wants per share of that same stock, and the spread is the difference between those two prices.

11. Close

The NYSE and Nasdaq close at 4 p.m., with after-hours trading continuing until 8 p.m. The close simply refers to the time at which a stock exchange closes to trading.

12. Day Trading

The practice of buying and selling within the same trading day, before the close of the markets on that day, is called day trading. This is my primary trading strategy, although I have a long-term portfolio, as well. Traders who participate in day trading are often called "active traders" or "day traders."

13. Dividend

A portion of a company's earnings that is paid to shareholders, or people that own that company's stock, on a quarterly or annual basis. Not all companies pay dividends. For instance, if you trade penny stocks, you're likely not after dividends.

14. Exchange

A place in which different investments are traded. The most well-known exchanges in the United States are the New York Stock Exchange (NYSE) and the Nasdaq.

15. Execution

When an order to buy or sell has been completed, the trader has executed the transaction. If you put in an order to sell 100 shares, this means that all 100 shares have been sold.

16. Haircut

In its simplest stock market terms, a haircut is an extremely thin spread between the bid and ask prices of a given stock. It can also refer to a situation in which a stock price gets reduced by a specific percentage for margin trades or other purposes.

17. High

A high refers to a market milestone in which a stock or index reaches a greater price point than previously. Record highs can signal that a stock or index has never reached the current price point, but there are also time-constrained highs, such as 30-day highs.

18. Index

A benchmark that is used as a reference marker for traders and portfolio managers. A 10 percent return may sound good, but if the market index returned 12 percent, then you didn't do very well since you could have just invested in an index fund and saved time by not trading frequently. Examples are the Dow Jones Industrial Average and Standard & Poor's 500.

19. Initial Public Offering (IPO)

An IPO is the first sale or offering of a stock by a company to the public. It happens when a company decides to go public rather than remain solely owned by private or inside investors. The Securities Exchange Commission (SEC) has strict rules that companies must follow before issuing an IPO.

20. Leverage

I'm not a fan of leverage, but it's good for you to know this stock market term. When you use leverage, you borrow shares in stock from your broker to increase your profit. If you borrow shares and sell them all at a higher price point, you return the shares and keep the difference. It's a dangerous game that I urge you to avoid playing.

21. Low

Low is the opposite of high. It represents a lower price point for a stock or index.

22. Margin

A margin account lets a person borrow money (take out a loan, essentially) from a broker to purchase an investment. The difference between the amount of the loan and the price of the securities is called the margin. Trading on margin can be dangerous because, if you're wrong about the direction in which the stock will go, you can lose significant cash. You must often maintain a minimum balance in a margin account.

23. Moving Average

A stock's average price-per-share during a specific period is called its moving average. Some common time frames to study in terms of a stock's moving average include 50- and 200-day moving averages.

24. Open

In the United States, the stock market opens at 9:30 a.m. Eastern time every day. It's based on the trading hours of the Nasdaq and NYSE. Pre-market trading hours begin at 4:30 a.m. Eastern, but most traders don't begin paying attention until about 8 a.m. Essentially, open refers to the time at which people can begin trading on a particular exchange.

25. Order

An investor's bid to buy or sell a certain amount of stock or option contracts constitutes an order. You have to put an order in to buy or sell 100 shares of stock, for instance.

26. Pink Sheet Stocks

The term "pink sheets" refers most commonly to penny stocks, which are traded at $5 per share or less. They're also called over-the-counter stocks because that's how they are traded. You won't find them on the Nasdaq or NYSE, or any other major exchange, and they're often smaller companies.

27. Portfolio

A collection of investments owned by an investor makes up his or her portfolio. You can have as few as one stock in a portfolio, but you can also own an infinite amount of stocks or other securities.

28. Quote

Information on a stock's latest trading price tells you its quote. This is sometimes delayed by 20 minutes unless you're using an actual broker trading platform.

29. Rally

A rapid increase in the general price level of the market or of the price of a stock is known as a rally. Depending on the overall environment, it might be called a bull rally or a bear rally. In a bear market, upward trends of as little as 10 percent can qualify as a rally.

30. Sector

A group of stocks that are in the same industry belongs to the same sector. An example would be the technology sector, which includes companies like Apple and Microsoft. Some traders prefer to trade in a specific sector, such as energy, because they know the industry well and can better predict stock price fluctuations.

31. Share Market

Any market in which shares of a particular company are bought and sold. The stock market is an example and probably the most significant example of a share market.

32. Short Selling

When you short-sell a stock, you borrow shares from someone else with the promise to return them at a point down the road. You then sell the stock for a profit. It's a way to take advantage of a stock that you believe will decrease in price. After you sell short, you can buy back the shares at a lower price point and take the difference in price as your profit.

33. Spread

This is the difference between the bid and the ask prices of a stock, or the amount for which someone is willing to buy it and the amount for which someone is willing to sell it. For instance, if a trader is willing to trade XYZ stock for $10 and a buyer is willing to pay $9 for it, the spread is $1.

34. Stock Symbol

A stock symbol is a one- to four-character alphabetic root symbol that represents a publicly-traded company on a stock exchange. Apple's stock symbol is AAPL, while Walmart's is WMT.

35. Volatility

The price movements of a stock or the stock market as a whole. Highly volatile stocks are those with extreme daily up and down movements and wide intraday trading ranges. This is often common with stocks that are thinly traded or have low trading volumes.

6. Volume

The number of shares of stock traded during a particular period, normally measured in average daily trading volume. Volume can also mean the number of shares you purchase of a given stock. For instance, buying 2,000 shares of a company is a higher-volume purchase than buying 20 shares.

37. Yield

Often refers to the measure of the return on an investment that is received from the payment of a dividend. This is determined by dividing the annual dividend amount by the price paid for the stock. If you bought stock XYZ for $40 per share and it pays a $1.00-per-year dividend, you have a "yield" of 2.5 percent.

Conclusion

Learning how to invest in stocks might take a little time, but you'll be on your way to building your wealth when you get the hang of it. Read various investment websites, test out different brokers and stock-trading apps, and diversify your portfolio to hedge against risk. Keep your risk tolerance and financial goals in mind, and you'll be able to call yourself a shareholder before you know it. You can make a lot of money investing in stocks or trading in the stock market, but it is not something for the new investors. Care must be taken when it comes to stock investments. The investor must have a solid understanding of stocks and how they trade in the market or risk losing money in a volatile type of investment.

Stocks are claims to a company's profit stream and are granted voting rights in installing its board of directors or in approving large corporate actions such as being acquired. Shareholders are not owners of a corporation's assets and do not involve themselves with corporate management. Stock is equity, bonds are debt. Bondholders are guaranteed a return on their investment and have a higher claim in recovery from bankruptcy than shareholders. This is generally why stocks are considered riskier investments and require a higher expected rate of return. You can lose all of your investments with stocks. The flip-side of this is you can make a lot of money if you invest in the right company.

The two main types of stock are common and preferred. It is also possible for a company to create different classes of stock. Stock markets are places where buyers and sellers of the stock meet to trade. Most trading takes place today via electronic trading. Stock market indexes give an overview of how the stock market is "doing." Stock prices change moment to moment according to supply and demand. There are many factors influencing prices, the most important of which are expectations about earnings. Still, there is no consensus as to why stock prices move the way they do.

To buy stocks you can either use a brokerage or a dividend reinvestment plan (DRIP). There are several different order types, and the type of order you use will depend on whether you are more concerned with price or with completing your order. Stock tables/quotes aren't that hard to read once you know what everything stands for! Bulls are optimistic and bull markets are defined by increasing stock prices. Bears are pessimists and bear markets occur when prices fall.

Understanding stock market return behavior is important for all countries. The degree of volatility present in the stock market leads investors to demand a higher risk premium, thereby creating higher capital cost, which impedes investment and slows economic development

Printed by Libri Plureos GmbH in Hamburg,
Germany

9 781801 886291